We Confess

We Confess

THE CHURCH

We Confess Series, Volume 3

Hermann Sasse

Translated by Norman Nagel

Publishing House
St. Louis

Contents

Translator's Preface 7

JESUS INTERCEDES FOR HIS CHURCH
 (1941/42) 11

ON THE DOCTRINE OF THE HOLY SPIRIT
 (July/August 1960) 17

ARTICLE VII OF THE AUGSBURG CONFESSION
IN THE PRESENT CRISIS OF LUTHERANISM
 (April 1961) 40

MINISTRY AND CONGREGATION
 (July 1949) 69

APOSTOLIC SUCCESSION
 (April 1956) 84

LAST THINGS: CHURCH AND ANTICHRIST
 (March 1952) 108

THE CHURCH LIVES!
 (June 27, 1943) 127

Translator's Preface

We begin and end with Sasse preaching. His preaching and theology are all of one piece, and he was no trimmer. There are things of first importance and others that are not, and Sasse is of enormous help in telling the difference. "Each sermon is more important than all those sessions which spend their time discussing big church resolutions regarding the Bonn constitution, the atom bomb, or Goethe's 200th birthday."

Dr. Sasse was a churchman, not a statesman. He did not market his message according to the mood of the moment or yesterday's social survey. He knew and loved the church and her history too profoundly. We do not invent or direct the church. We are to preach what we have been given to preach, "the forgiveness and justification of sinners for Christ's sake."

For His church Christ prays. The church can no more be destroyed than Christ can be destroyed. With this confidence it is possible to face squarely what would destroy the church. Most damaging are the attacks from within, the subversion of the Gospel to the uses of power to make of the church a political force, ruled by the decisions of men. Such decisions may claim episcopal, synodical, papal, presbyterial, or congregational authority. No claim holds except it be of Christ, the Holy Spirit, and His Scripture.

Two sermons and five letters are what we have in this book, with their matter rather than their dates determining the sequence. The dates, however, are important, and with them Sasse's specific message. The first sermon was preached to a small congregation celebrating the anniversary of the dedication of its church. It was during the war, when the comforting message that "Jesus prays for His church" was particularly needed.

The letter on the Holy Spirit was written after Sasse had been in Adelaide 11 years. His grasp of the intimate connection between the doctrine and the history of the church, which had thrilled the packed lecture hall in Erlangen, moved deeper to the intimate connection between the believer and Christ, His Spirit, and His church. Sasse grieved for the loss of students, so gifted, so promising, killed in the war. With faith's "nevertheless" he carries forward the work of one of the most brilliant of his students, "meaninglessly" killed in the war. He tells us the name, and speaks of those too whose names are known only to the Lord, " . . . somewhere in China." God the Holy Spirit "brings the uncompleted work to completion."

Dr. Sasse was above all a confessional theologian, and therefore confessing the faith was of the greatest importance for him. So it is fitting that we hear what he has to say about the relevance of the Augsburg Confession's famous Article VII ("The Church") for the worldwide Lutheran Church of today.

In the 19th century the great Lutheran churchmen Walther and Löhe were unable to agree on the doctrine of church and ministry and therefore sadly went their separate ways. In Australia Dr. Sasse was able to bring together the two streams of Lutheranism which might be characterized as emanating from these two theological giants. His letter on "Ministry and Congregation" is an effort toward the same conjunction in America. Although we know the subsequent sad history, this does not rob the letter of its importance.

When our confidence does not live from what has been given to the church, then we are tempted to add things to make it more sure. Sasse gives the history of the notion of apostolic succession, and its roots in men's efforts to guarantee the church. He recalls us to the grounds of confidence which alone finally hold.

In light of this the final letter, "Last Things: Church and Antichrist," speaks for itself. There are facts to be faced, documented, and honestly dealt with "in these last days." There are confessional tasks that may not be shirked.

Sasse was a confessor involved. In 1927 he played a leading role in the World Conference on Faith and Order in Lausanne. When the Nazis kept his passport, he could no longer carry forward this involvement. He was a leading theologian involved in working toward Barmen. But in the night of May 30, 1934, he left Barmen when he was denied the opportunity to speak on the morrow. Those who were arranging things did not wish to hear him further (*Die lutherischen Kirchen und die Bekenntnissynode von Barmen*, ed. W. Hauschild, p. 98).

After the war, finding the confessional situation of Lutheranism in Germany most deplorable, He left Erlangen and eventually accepted a call to Immanuel Seminary in Adelaide, Australia, where he continued to write his "Letters to Lutheran Pastors." There are points in them where pain, anger, and passion burn through. Then it is well to remember that only as sinners forgiven for Christ's sake can any of us carry on our work. There is something to trouble everyone in Sasse. This can be avoided by simply ignoring him, or by listening only when he agrees with us. To listen when he says unwelcome things may prove most fruitful. This is not to say that he is always right, as neither are any of us. Rather it points to his helpfulness in drawing us into always deeper probing, testing, and appropriation of Christian truth.

Sasse's last words to us in this volume are from the pulpit. "When the day comes when this war is over . . . " In a situation in which there appeared to be nothing but doom, he preached about the ongoing true life of the church. He proclaimed: "Nations pass away, but the church continues . . . because the future of the church is the future of Jesus Christ. Amen."

JESUS INTERCEDES FOR HIS CHURCH

A sermon on John 17:6–23 during the war (1941/42)
for the anniversary of the dedication
of a church and a meeting
of the Martin Luther Bund

How inexhaustible the abundance of Holy Scripture! There are texts there that a man could spend his whole life studying without exhausting their depths. Yes, the labor of many centuries on the part of Christendom is required to understand such passages fully. For 1,500 years the church read the epistles of the apostle Paul to the Romans and the Galatians. Faithful Christians were nourished by them in the church service. They were explored by profoundly learned men, from the ancient church fathers to the masters of medieval theology. Then after 15 centuries the hour came when the depths of their doctrine of justification were laid bare in the Reformation.

Perhaps something similar may happen with the great texts of the Bible which speaks of the divine mystery of the church: the Epistle of Paul to the Ephesians, and this great 17th chapter of the Gospel According to St. John. August Vilmar, the great Lutheran theologian of the 19th century, repeatedly expressed the hope that out of the severe struggles of the church, out of what Christians were living through in his day, there might grow a full understanding of what the New Testament says of the church. If this could be learned, he said, such a new understanding of the Third Article might be as great a turning point in the history of the church as was the new understanding of the Second Article in the Reformation.

Our celebration today of the anniversary of the dedication of this church gives us the opportunity to ponder and probe what our text says of the mystery of the church. This is given us as we stand engaged in a great struggle for the sake of the church. Your house of God has stood here now for more than 30 years. Compared with the age of other churches that is a very short time.

11

Our text speaks to us about the miracle of the church's preservation. The preservation of the church is no smaller miracle than its founding, just as the preservation of the world is no smaller miracle than its creation. It is by no means self-evident that the church should continue. In whole regions of the world it has almost or completely gone under. Many a people among whom there was a flourishing church has rejected this church. There is no sadder sight than the ruins of old churches, such as may be seen in parts of Asia which have sunk back into heathenism.

No lesser man than Martin Luther reckoned with the possibility that the church might one day be taken from our people. "God's Word and grace is like rain which falls on one place and then goes on to fall on another, not returning again to where it once was before." He pointed to those lands which once were a part of ancient Christendom but which sank back again into heathenism, and he spoke the warning: "You Germans must not imagine that it will be yours forever. Unthankfulness and scorn of it will not let it remain."

No, it is not self-evident that the church will remain where it once has been. To the whole church of Christ the promise is indeed given that the gates of hell shall not prevail against it, but this is not something that any congregation or particular church can say of itself. Just as an individual Christian may fall away, so also whole congregations, whole parts of the church, may fall away. We can read of this already in the New Testament.

No, it is not self-evident that the church will abide. That was known also by Him who speaks in our Gospel: Jesus Christ, the Lord, in the night in which He was betrayed. What He said to His disciples in that farewell night He now says once more. But He does not say it to men, but to His heavenly Father.

The final care that moves Him is His care for His church. His work on earth is completed. "I have manifested Thy name to the men whom Thou gavest Me out of the world." " I have given them the words which Thou gavest Me." "I have given them Thy Word." And this Word was not without fruit. "They have kept Thy Word." "They have received [it] and know in truth that I came from Thee; and they have believed that Thou didst send Me." And this faith held. "While I was with them I kept them in Thy name. . . . I have guarded them, and none of them is lost but the son of perdition, that the Scripture might be fulfilled." "While I was with them"—as long as that was the case there was no need to worry about the future of the Gospel. But now that He is coming to the Father, Jesus says: "I am no more in the world, but they are in the world."

Now, however, they would no longer hear His lovely voice or look into His eyes. What would become of them? Never has such a task been given to men as was given to the apostles by their Lord at His farewell. To this little flock, the Eleven, a responsibility was given such as was never laid on any others. "As Thou didst send Me into the world, so I have sent them into the world."

Should they fail, what would then become of the Gospel? And were they really the men who were equal to this task? "Then all the disciples forsook Him and fled"; so we are told about their behavior that same night (Matt. 26:56). "I do not know the man"; so said Simon Peter (Matt. 26:72), the same Peter who made the first confession and whom Jesus therefore called blessed (Matt. 16:17). To such men as these the great work is entrusted which Jesus leaves behind: "As the Father has sent Me, even so I send you" (John 20:21).

Yes, it is these feeble men whom He sends, men who do not have any more faith than any of us. They are men who do not possess the natural gifts that would be necessary to win the hearts of humankind. And He sends them into a world that does not want to know anything about them or their message. "And now I am no more in the world, but they are in the world." "And the world has hated them because they are not of the world, even as I am not of the world." That world will not take long to finish them off! If the world can nail Him to the cross, won't it be able to dispose of this handful of men?

Jesus sees that all quite clearly. How could He have any illusions about His disciples—especially in that night? In that situation He does one thing: *He prays for them.* "I am praying for them; I am not praying for the world but for those whom Thou hast given Me, for they are Thine." "Holy Father, keep them in Thy name, which Thou hast given Me, that they may be one, even as We are one." "I do not pray that Thou shouldst take them out of the world, but that Thou shouldst keep them from the evil one." "Sanctify them in the truth . . . that they also may be consecrated in truth."

Jesus prays for them. He moves from farewell discourse with His disciples to farewell prayer. Now He speaks no more to men but to His heavenly Father. Here in this great chapter of the Gospel According to John we have the greatest of all prayers. Here it is not a mere man who is praying—no human being can pray it after Him. Here prays the eternal Son. All other prayers are prayers of men to God, prayers of creatures to their Creator. But this one prayer is prayed by the eternal Son to the Father. He, the High Priest, utters it for His church. He who is on the way to Golgotha, He speaks it: "For their sake I consecrate Myself, that they also may be consecrated in truth." And He does not think only of His apostles. Rather He looks further than the farthest times of the church's history, over all generations, over all the centuries to the end of the world: "I do not pray for these alone, but also for those who will believe in Me through their word" [NKJV]. He prays for the preservation of the church. And this prayer is heard. That is the secret of the church's preservation.

We will understand this better if we ponder what is the meaning of intercession in our lives—or what it should be. There is nothing that so holds and carries our children as the intercession we make for them. There also is nothing that more deeply binds parents and children together. There would be far less anxiety about our children if we would lay all our cares for them on the father heart of God. There is nothing that so binds husband and wife together, that so helps them bear each other's burdens, as the intercessions they make for each other.

There also is nothing in the church which so binds its members together as interceding for one another. When for years on end the apostle Paul sat in prison while his mission congregations were left without protection, helpless in the world, there yet remained this one thing that he could do for them: "For this reason I bow my knees before the Father, from whom every family in heaven and on earth is named . . . " (Eph. 3:14–15). This prayer broke through the walls of the prison, and bound the apostle and his congregations together.

Therefore we make intercession in the church also for our people and government, for all who are in need and temptation, for the sick and the dying, for the church of God throughout the whole world. We remember our brethren in the diaspora. We think of the Lutheran Church of Brazil, which has such close ties with the Martin Luther Bund and our church here in Franconia. We recall our German brothers in Australia, who have remained such faithful friends of the old homeland because the Lutheran Church has preserved the German language for them through the Bible, the Catechism, the hymnbook, and the liturgy. We think of those isolated Germans who today bow their knees with us in villages in the Kirgiz Republic [of the Soviet Union] or in the forests of Siberia. We remember all brethren in the faith, including the missionaries in prison. Today, when we are separated from them by more than land and ocean, and can no longer give them any external help, we know what is the power of intercession.

If that is so of the intercession which we human beings make for one another here on earth, how much more powerful is that intercession which the Head of the church makes for His members. His prayer will truly and certainly be heard. He prays for us. "I have prayed for you that your faith may not fail" (Luke 22:32). That prayer rescued Peter.

"I do not pray for these alone, but also for those who will believe in Me through their word" [NKJV]. In this prayer we too are included, you and I and every Christian who sets his entire confidence on Jesus Christ as his Savior.

Christ prays for us, and His prayer is heard. This comes to expression in the liturgy when, before the Collect, we chant: "The Lord be with you"—and then the response, "And with your spirit." [We are saying:] "May the Lord be with you as you now pray—and may He be with your spirit as you now speak out our prayer." Jesus Christ is praying along with us. The church prays together with her Head. And this prayer is heard "through Jesus Christ, our Lord."

He prays for us. He prays for His church on earth. This is the miracle of the church's preservation. Hear Luther's confession of this fact:

> It is not we who are able to maintain the church, nor could those before us, nor will those who come after us be able to do so. It is only He who says, "Lo, I am with you always, to the close of the age." It has always been He, is He now, and will always be He. As it is written in Heb. 13, "Jesus Christ is the same yesterday and today and forever." And Rev. 1, " . . . who is and who was and who is to come." He is the Man. That is His name, which belongs to no other man, nor may it be given to any other.

Oh, if one could only believe this! Oh, if we would but learn something from this great and childlike trust of Luther's! How much less would cares for the church oppress us if we would only cast all our cares upon Him who has taken the care of the church upon Himself. How differently we would then do what He bids us do for the sake of the preservation of His church.

Only when we have this great faith in Him who wondrously preserves His church, only then do we know how the church is sustained. How is the church on earth sustained? "Sanctify them in the truth; Thy Word is truth." "Through the Word the church was brought into existence; through the Word the church is preserved." So Luther once said.

As the Word founded the church—"I have given them Thy Word"—so the Word of Christ preserves the church. Not the most brilliant of human organizing, not the most splendid liturgy, not the wisest of men, not the most splendid church buildings preserve the church. It is done by the Word alone, by the plain Word of the Gospel as the saving message of the forgiveness of sins. "Fruitful ethics can be found also in Confucianism, a resplendent hierarchy also with the Dalai Lama, scientific theology also in the synagogue, a battle against alcohol also among the Turks, and a youth movement also in Moscow—forgiveness of sins alone with Jesus Christ."

The Word of forgiveness which only Jesus Christ can speak, because it is He who has borne the sin of the world, the Word of forgiveness His church is to speak as it follows Him—that is the Gospel. And it is this Word that creates the unity of the church, the unity of all the children of God. "Where this article remains pure and active, there the church remains in fine unity. Where this article does not remain pure there is no defense against a single error or any Enthusiasm." Therefore take care that this may be the case!

In our care for those in the diaspora we have learned that everything depends on the Word, on the pure proclamation of the Gospel. That is the greatest service we can perform for the preservation of the church. Father Löhe was much mocked and resisted in his day when he began his great work for those in the diaspora by training messengers in the pure doctrine. The congregations he founded in America have to this day remained watchmen of the Gospel. In this way we also belong to the great communion of the church of all ages, along with the fathers who made confession before us, along with the teachers of the church, along with the apostles—" . . . that they may be one . . . I in them and Thou in Me."

To know this is to know something of the church. The time will come when the Third Article of the Creed will be understood. The question of the church will be one of the great questions of the future. What a blessed secret this article of faith contains, what a miracle God's church is—all this can only be known by those who themselves are among those for whom Jesus Christ prayed: "Holy Father, keep them in Thy name, which Thou hast given Me. . . . Sanctify them in the truth; Thy Word is truth."

And so we then pray to Him: "Lord Jesus Christ, have mercy on us. You are the Deliverer of Your church, the Savior of Your body. Amen."

ON THE DOCTRINE OF THE HOLY SPIRIT

Letters to Lutheran Pastors, No. 51
July/August 1960

This letter should have arrived for Pentecost—but then in the church it is always Pentecost, or should be. Every Sunday is not only an Easter day but also a little Pentecost. So perhaps my greetings to you are not too late. The doctrine of the Holy Spirit, which will engage us here, lies behind all the questions and all the needs of the church and the holy ministry which concern us day by day. As we ponder several dogmatic and historical questions in regard to this doctrine, may it be of help to us all.

1

"The true doctrine of the Holy Spirit has no place to call its own in the church and congregation. It appears to have become a foreign body. This state of affairs must be recognized quite objectively." With these words Otto Henning Nebe began his thesis (*Habilitationsschrift*) for the University of Erlangen, *Deus Spiritus Sanctus* (*Beiträge zur Förderung christlicher Theologie, Band* 40, *Heft* 5, 1939). He was one of our most promising young doctors of theology but was killed in the war. His small but thoughtful document has not received the attention it deserves. Even so, we should not ignore the warning given with these opening words of his.

If indeed the true doctrine of the Holy Spirit has lost its place (*Heimatrecht*) in church and congregation, then it cannot be long before the reality of the Holy Spirit is also lost to us, just as Christ ceases to be present when He is not truly taught, when His Gospel and sacraments are falsified. Here may lie the explanation of the decline of those means in the church which are to be the specific locations of the activity of the Holy Spirit.

Think of the needs of the office of the ministry! How can we explain the shortage of pastors in so many churches of every confession? Why do those young men who in other times would have become pastors now turn to secular callings? Why do pastors now find that their office has become a problem—and not only in Germany, where everything becomes a problem? How are we to explain the high number of nervous breakdowns among Protestant pastors that are reported to be happening in America? How are we to explain the increasing number of women pastors in the Protestant world—and the theological incompetence, even among Lutherans, in giving an answer to this comparatively simple problem, when every confirmand knows the answer?

We are all aware of the demands and pressures laid on our office. In churches nowadays the pastor has to do so many things which do not really belong to his office, that he scarcely has time for his real office, "the ministry of teaching the Gospel and administering the sacraments" [Augsburg Confession V; Tappert, p. 31]. In Germany I knew superintendents and deans who were so frazzled by the work of the week that only on Saturday evening did they finally come to sermon preparation.

We hear something of this already in an article by August Vilmar in 1849, entitled "Power over the Spirits." He spoke of where all this would lead, all this external business, all the meetings of church groups, all this having to get the money together. Deacons are to have the responsibility for such things. They are not to draw a pastor away from what he is called to do as a pastor. Vilmar preached to deaf ears, this great pastor of pastors, for whom a consistorialized church had no place. The process of the secularization of the holy ministry was not halted by all the rethinking of the nature of the office after World War I, nor even by the Church Struggle (*Kirchenkampf*) in Germany. In pondering all this we may catch a glimpse of what a church still knows of the activity of the Holy Spirit.

What is happening with the holy ministry shows what is wrong with us. We seek the Holy Spirit where He is not to be found. We no longer find Him where He would be found. We speak of Him, but our faith in Him, in His deity, in His divine Person, has grown weak, or has even been lost. If things continue to go on like this, the outcome for our church is only too clear.

2

We modern Christians seek the Holy Spirit where He is not to be found. In doing this we are, however, certainly not the first. This is a danger which has always been there since the days of the apostles, and ever and again there have been Christians, indeed whole churches, that have fallen victim to it. In the second century there was Montanism. The question which then deeply troubled Christianity and divided it was whether it was actually the Holy Spirit, the Paraclete, who was revealing Himself in the new prophesyings. We may recall the spiritualistic Franciscans in the Middle Ages, the Enthusiast movements of the *Schwärmer* against whom Luther had to battle, and in our day the various Pentecostal movements. Earnest Christians have often felt compelled to admit what leading men in the Fellowship Movement, who once acknowledged the Pentecostal Movement's speaking in tongues, which had gone on since 1905, came to recognize: It was not the Holy Spirit.

We are now not speaking of this danger, but of the frivolous manner in which we in the modern world speak of the experience of the Holy Spirit. The roots of this are in the English Enthusiasm of the 17th century and in the Pietism and Methodism of the 18th century. When at the Berlin *Kirchentag* of 1853 in a profoundly untruthful declaration the participants declared themselves loyal to the Augsburg Confession "with heart and mouth," but also with the reservation that the unity of the confession they were making was not to be injured by the differing views on its Article X that were held by the Lutherans, the Reformed, and those from Union churches, this uniting of Evangelical Germany was regarded by many as a work of the Holy Spirit. It has become almost customary at great church gatherings, and also at the big ecumenical gatherings, to perceive and solemnly proclaim the blowing of the Holy Spirit. A sort of new Pentecost is experienced in the singing of great hymns in many languages. We need to consider the mass psychology which is going on in such big gatherings, especially at a time when the world's techniques for manipulating a crowd and its modern communications media are penetrating the church.

What is said here is not spoken against getting things organized as such, nor against the way news can now go round the world, nor against the means of communication provided by modern technology. Of such things Vilmar already observed that they are there not only for the children of this world, but are also to be brought into the service of Christ's church. But we are asking whether we are always aware that there can be mass psychoses also in the church. When the church does take for its use the techniques which can control or lead a crowd of people, then there is the most urgent need to pray for that great gift of grace, the discerning and the testing of the spirits.

We seek the Holy Spirit where He is not to be found when we take it as self-evident that the way our church is developing is altogether due to the guidance of the Holy Spirit. This is not only Rome's great error; it is an error found also in other churches. The "Message" of the Lambeth Conference of 1958 begins with the statement that the bishops there assembled wished to share with all members of their church in the world the experience "which has come to us, in a fresh and wonderful way, by the power of God's Spirit among us." "We ourselves have been knit together by the Holy Spirit in mutual understanding and trust." "Because we ourselves have been thus drawn together, God has given us a message of reconciliation for the Church and the world." This message then begins with the statement: "A divided Church cannot heal the wounds of a divided world." Then God is thanked "that in Asia and Africa, as well as in Britain and America, Christian Churches are actively moving towards a greater measure of unity" (*Report*, pp. 1, 29). There is then nothing to wonder at in the answer given at a press conference by an Anglican bishop. He was asked why the Lambeth Conference, which had previously rejected birth control, had now approved it. He answered that it was by the guidance of the Holy Spirit! At Lambeth, then, the Holy Spirit is said to have confirmed the Anglican understanding of the church as well as the unionism in India and America. What has happened here to the Biblical: "It has seemed good to the Holy Spirit and to us . . ." [Acts 15:28]? The same miracle is said to have occurred at the Barmen synod in 1934, where Karl Barth's *Bekenntnisunion* was approved, and the Lutherans, the Reformed, and those of the Union churches declared that "they sought a common message for the need and temptation of the church in our day. With gratitude to God they surely believe that a common message has been put into their mouth" (Schmidt II, 92; Cochrane, *The Church's Confession Under Hitler*, p. 237). What has happened here to "Behold, I have put My words in your mouth" (Jer. 1:9; cf. Deut. 18:18)?

What Luther has to say about all this may be found in the Smalcald Articles:

> All this is the old devil and the old serpent who made enthusiasts of Adam and Eve. He led them from the external Word of God to spiritualizing and to their own imaginations, and he did this through other external words. . . . In short, enthusiasm clings to Adam and his descendants from the beginning to the end of the world. It is a poison

implanted and inoculated in man by the old dragon, and it is the source, strength, and power of all heresy, including that of the papacy and Mohammedanism" (SA III, VIII, 5 and 9).

"It is the source, strength, and power . . . of the papacy." It is a very serious question, if we really have to choose among the Enthusiasms which go on among Christians, whether the Roman one is not perhaps the lesser evil. Rome's decisions are at least based on thorough and learned consultation, and they let the ancient doctrine stand.

3

We seek the Holy Spirit where He is not to be found when we take it as self-evident that He has to come with every sermon we preach. God's Word indeed has the promise: "It shall not return to Me empty" [Is. 55:11]. But we must always ask ourselves whether what we preach is in fact God's Word. When the sermon is a true exposition of the Scriptural text, then, in spite of all our weakness, God's Word is preached. But how many sermons are preached, also in Lutheran churches, where the Gospel is not taught fully and clearly!

We seem to suppose that it is enough to train young men for four or five years. They pass their examinations more or less adequately. They are ordained and sent to some field of service. They may gather some people who do not belong to any church, but who are interested in religious questions. These then form a congregation that receives the rights of a Lutheran congregation without understanding the Catechism or the Augsburg Confession. The same thing happens in the European churches. Young candidates equipped with Bultmann's theology are sent to the sprawling suburbs of our large cities. Or they are sent into the country, where the farmers and laborers may be fortunate enough not to understand what the young man believes, or does not believe. Do we really suppose the Holy Spirit will all by Himself build a church and congregation there? He can of course make use of such instruments too. "The Word of God is not fettered" (2 Tim. 2:9), and many a pastor has been brought to the Gospel by his congregation. Many who did not understand the Gospel and the sacraments have learned in the desert of their own theological existence what the university did not teach them. But that such things happen in the mercy of God does not relieve us of having to be quite clear about what kind of a proclamation it is to which the promise has been given that through it the Holy Spirit comes to the souls of men.

Finally, we seek the Holy Spirit where He is not to be found, when we overlook the fact that while the Holy Spirit is indeed given in correct preaching, He does not always create faith, but only "where and when it pleases God." This is the teaching of the Augsburg Confession (Art. V, 2 [Tappert, p. 31]). It is not changed by the fact that under Barth's influence the "where and when it pleases God" has been misunderstood as though it meant that the Holy Spirit has not bound Himself to the Word and that God's freedom consisted in this, that He makes the preached or written Word into the Word of God for one person but not for another. [Thence the view that it *is* not the Word of God, but may *become* the Word of God.] Against this we must hold firmly that the external Word of Scripture and correct Scriptural preaching always brings the Holy Spirit. But we must never forget the other truth, that the Holy Spirit does not always work faith. This is *the freedom of God the Holy Spirit* which Article V of the Augsburg Confession teaches.

The doctrine of grace of the Reformers is a measurement of how far modern Protestantism has fallen away from the Reformation. Whatever their differences were in the doctrine of election, Luther and Calvin were agreed that it simply does not lie within the power of man to accept the grace of God or not. Already in the 17th century "by grace alone" (*sola gratia*) began losing ground among the Reformed (Arminianism) and Lutherans (election *intuitu fidei*, "in view of a person's believing later on"). How deeply this new form of synergism had penetrated the Lutheranism of the 19th century is evidenced by the failure to recognize even today what was at stake in the controversy over the election of grace, in which the Missouri Synod in America contended for *sola gratia* as confessed by Luther. The optimism and synergism prevalent in America have made such inroads into American Lutheranism that the Augsburg Confession's "where and when it pleases God" has for practical purposes been given up.

Evidence of this is the uncritical taking over of ideas and programs of stewardship and evangelism from such groups as the Seventh Day Adventists. The pastor schools his people so that with the right kind of pious talk they will then be equipped to win other people for the church. In place of the office of preaching reconciliation comes the training of "soul winners," teaching them just the right way of talking with people, to make maximum use of the techniques of psychological manipulation. The system admittedly derives from the methods of American business. Thus people are to be brought into the church, made to feel at home there, be led to make a decision, and then all together they are to carry on their building of the kingdom of God. What the Word of God is no longer trusted to do is achieved with the psychological techniques of such modern evangelization. There is of course talk of the Holy Spirit, but one no longer knows who He is. It seems He can be measured and quantified. Such evangelism produces results. Thousands are won for church membership. On the other hand we may recall the failure of the Biblical prophets and of our Lord Himself. When one considers the latter, one begins to understand the full earnestness of the "where and when it pleases God." Jesus said: " . . . so that they may indeed see but not perceive, and may indeed hear but not understand; lest they should turn again, and be forgiven" (Mark 4:12; cf. Is. 6:9–10). Whoever is not awed by what is hidden deep in these words will never truly know the Holy Spirit.

4

We modern people no longer find the Holy Spirit where He would be sought. This has been true to a certain extent throughout the church's history, ever since the days when it was necessary for Paul to teach the church in Corinth that the quiet workings of the Holy Spirit are His greatest ones. But it is especially true of us, who no longer understand *the bond of the Holy Spirit with the external means of grace* and perhaps do not even want to hear of it anymore.

Article V of the Augsburg Confession states: "Condemned are the Anabaptists and others who teach that the Holy Spirit comes to us through our own preparations, thoughts, and works without the external word of the Gospel." Now the spiritualizers, no matter of what period, will surely deny that they seek to get the Spirit by their own preparation and works. But they deceive themselves. The "preparation" is an essential part of such "spiritual" experience, and involves some doing on the part of man. This may be observed in the directions given by the great masters of mysticism, in the way a Quaker meeting waits in holy silence, or in Thomas Münzer's self-chosen cross by which he would compel the inner word to come.

Luther saw all this with remarkable clarity, as may be seen in his classic statement on "Confession" in the Smalcald Articles [III, VIII; Tappert, pp. 312—13]. The Spirit cannot be separated from the Word, just as in Holy Scripture *logos* and *pneuma* cannot be separated, although one must distinguish between them. As the eternal Word and the Spirit of God were involved in Creation (Gen. 1:2; John 1:1–3; cf.

1 Cor. 8:5–6), so in all the great deeds of God, the Son and the Spirit belong together: in the Incarnation ("who was conceived by the Holy Spirit"), at the baptism of Jesus, and at His resurrection (1 Tim. 3:16). Here is the inner reason for the Holy Spirit's bonding Himself (as far as we are concerned) with the external words of Scripture and their preaching. He who in John 3:8 is likened to the wind that "blows where it wills" has in His freedom as Lord ("And I believe in the Holy Spirit, the Lord") bound Himself to the external means of grace, so that we may know where we can find Him. For this reason, Luther explains, the spiritualizers, who want to have the Spirit without the external means of grace, make up their own means of grace. "Even so, the enthusiasts of our day condemn the external Word, yet they do not remain silent but fill the world with their chattering and scribbling, as if the Spirit could not come through the Scriptures or the spoken word of the apostles but must come through their own writings and words" (Smalcald Articles III, VIII, 6).

The profound truth of these words is evidenced throughout history. At the beginning of this century there appeared *Religious Voices of the Peoples*. It was a time of great historical research into the books of the Bible, and yet in German Protestantism understanding of the Bible had reached its nadir. The "religious voices" were those of the classical writings of the great religions of Asia. In cultured society they became books of edification and a means for achieving the "religious experience" which the church could no longer provide. At that time Oswald Spengler made his telling comment about the modern man who, instead of taking his hymnbook and going to church, stayed at home and read Confucius on rice paper.

Everywhere we seek the Holy Spirit, only not there where He is to be found. And why not? We feel it is unworthy of the Holy Spirit to bind Himself to such unimpressive external means as the homely words of Scripture, the words of Scripture interpretation, the lowly water of Baptism. "How can water produce such great effects?" we ask. To this the Small Catechism replies: "It is not the water indeed that produces these effects, but the Word of God connected with the water" [IV, 9–10]. But we ask: "How can the lowly water in Baptism convey the Holy Spirit?" It seems beneath the dignity of the Holy Spirit to be bonded with something so elementary as water and the physical sound of human words.

Zwingli expressed this thought in contradiction to Luther when he laid down the principle that bodily eating and drinking can be of no benefit to the soul. "The soul 'eats' spirit, and therefore it does not eat flesh" [*This Is My Body*, 1977, p. 193]. The humanism and idealism of modern man are speaking through him, while Luther resolutely holds to the fundamental Biblical concept of a real incarnation. "The Word became flesh." The Spirit comes in the external words of Scripture. In the Lord's Supper the bread is the body of Christ, and the wine His blood—not only sign or symbol. This essence of the Biblical revelation is perhaps the hardest thing we modern Christians, also we Lutherans, must learn again. We are so accustomed to think of body and soul, flesh and spirit, as opposites that we no longer understand that the whole magnitude of God's love lies in this very fact that God's Son comes to us in the flesh and that the Holy Spirit binds Himself to the external means of grace.

As God outside of Christ always remains the hidden God, so His Holy Spirit remains hidden from us unless we find Him in the Word and in the sacraments. And just as the revelation of God in Christ is at the same time God's hiding in the human nature of Christ, so the Holy Spirit of God is deeply hidden in the means of grace. He is always an object of faith, not of sight. "I believe that by my own reason or strength I cannot believe in Jesus Christ, my Lord, or come to him; but the Holy Spirit has called me through the Gospel, enlightened me with his gifts . . . " [Small Catechism II, 6]. Similarly we cannot believe in the Holy Spirit except by the witness He gives of Himself in God's Word. There both are found, the Son and the Spirit. There the Spirit witnesses to the Son of God (1 Cor. 12:3). There the Son bears witness to the Holy Spirit (see the words of the Lord about the Paraclete in John 14—16).

Without the Gospel, without the apostolic witness about Christ, we would be like those disciples in Acts 19:1–7 who had only received John's baptism and did not know "that there is a Holy Spirit." We might then know of the Holy Spirit as a force, a divine power that comes upon certain people, but we would not know that He is God. Only he who confesses in the Second Article that the Son is "God of God, Light of Light, very God of very God, begotten not made, being of one substance with the Father . . . " can go on to confess the faith of the Third Article: I believe "in the Holy Spirit, the lord and giver of life, who proceeds from the Father and the Son: who together with the Father and the Son is worshiped and glorified: who spoke by the prophets" [Tappert, p. 18, 19].

5

The Holy Spirit wants to be found in the Word. There He reveals Himself to us as God, as very God. Our faith in the Holy Spirit has grown weak. We seem to regard Him as a power of God, but no longer as a person. That He is more than the power of God that comes over man we learn from our Lord Himself. Without the promises about the Paraclete one could perhaps take the passages in the Old and the New Testament that speak of the Spirit in that sense. This is the case especially since the Greek *Pneuma Hagion* is in the neuter, and not in the masculine like the Latin *Spiritus Sanctus*. The Hebrew ruach is in the feminine. This suggests the difficulty our human words have in expressing the divine mystery of the Holy Spirit. In the Farewell Discourse in John, the Holy Spirit is called the Paraclete. "If I go, I will send Him (*auton*) to you. And when He (*ekeinos*) comes, He will convince the world . . . " (16:7–8; cf. the following verses and 14:26; 15:26). That this is not just Johannine is shown by Jesus' words about blasphemy against the Holy Spirit [Mark 3:29]. Blasphemy against the Holy Spirit is more than blasphemy against a something; it is blasphemy against a person, as the juxtaposition of "Son of Man" and "Holy Spirit" shows [Matt. 12:32; Luke 12:10]. And this person is God.

God's Word witnesses to the fact that the Holy Spirit is very God, or to be more exact, God the Holy Spirit witnesses to Himself in the words of Scripture, and nowhere else. This makes clear, then, how closely the understanding of Scripture as the Word of God hangs together with the right understanding of the Holy Spirit as a divine Person. Here is one of the reasons why we have lost the correct doctrine of the inspiration of Holy Scripture. If Scripture is no longer God's Word, then the Holy Spirit is no longer a divine Person. And vice versa: Whoever does not understand the Spirit as a divine Person, but as a *motus in rebus creatus* ("a movement which is produced in things"), as the Augsburg Confession speaks of this error in Article I [Tappert, p. 28], also no longer understands Scripture as God's Word but as a collection of religious writings that may stir a sense of something divine, "a breath of the divine." As Goethe said about the gospels in his last conversation with Eckermann: "There is in them the reflection of a majesty that emanates from the person of Christ. Here is as eminently divine a quality as can be found in any appearance ever of the divine on earth."

The development of Protestant theology since the Enlightenment shows clearly that the decline of belief in Scripture as the Word of God goes hand in hand with the decline of belief in the Holy Spirit as a divine Person. We can observe this also today, even where it is supposed that the old Liberalism has been overcome. What does the Holy Spirit mean for Gogarten, to cite just one example? If we read his book on *The Proclamation of Jesus Christ* (1948), we will find evidence enough for what has just been said. Where the doctrine of the Person of the Holy Spirit is no longer rightly taught, there also the doctrine of the Person of Christ is no longer rightly understood. The fathers of the fourth century knew this very well, and that brings us to one of the most difficult problems in the history of doctrine, one that is of more than just historical interest.

6

In studying the doctrine of inspiration in the fathers up to Augustine and Gregory the Great, one cannot escape the question: "Why did these theologians, when they came to speak of the relationship between Scripture and the Spirit, always draw their ideas from the Hellenistic synagogue?" These ideas, as becomes quite clear in Philo, go back to heathen concepts about the inspiration of prophets, sibyls, and the Sibylline Books. This matter was taken up years ago in these letters in "Augustine's Doctrine of Inspiration" (No. 29; also *Festschrift für Franz Dornseiff*, 1953, p. 262 ff.). Why did the fathers not simply say the same as Scripture says about its origin, the same thing our Lord Himself said (Matt. 22:43; John 5:39; 10:35), as well as His apostles (Acts 1:16; 2 Tim. 3:16; 2 Peter 1:19–21). Instead they tried to describe the process of inspiration in terms of ancient psychology.

We must realize that all the well-known ideas and pictures that have been in use since Augustine and Gregory to describe inspiration (the "prompting" or "dictating" of the Spirit, the holy writers as "secretaries" or "pens," etc.) derive from the psychology current in late antiquity, which could know nothing of the Holy Spirit. Just as the Holy Spirit Himself is inaccessible to any psychology, so also are His workings. Psychology may indeed examine certain psychological data, such as those connected with conversions. It can also examine certain phenomena of religious Enthusiasm. The proper work of the Holy Spirit, however, lies beyond what any psychology can explain or describe: regeneration, how the genuine prophets experienced God, what God's Word and the sacraments of Christ do in the human soul. The doctrine of the inspiration of Scripture which the church confesses must be a part of the doctrine of the Holy Spirit, but such a doctrine was not yet there when the fathers struggled with the problem of inspiration.

We seldom recall how long it took until the Scriptural doctrine of the Holy Spirit was understood. Something similar may be said of the doctrine of Christ. This doctrine was there from the beginning, ever since Jesus asked His disciples, "Who do you say that I am?" [Matt. 16:15]. But it took centuries until Christendom realized what all was included in the simple confessions, "Jesus is the Christ," "Jesus Christ is Lord," "I believe that Jesus Christ is the Son of God," and until the church recognized which wrong ideas had to be rejected if faith in Christ were not to be lost. It took even longer before clarity was achieved as to the full meaning of what Scripture says about the Holy Spirit.

Meanwhile Christians were being baptized "In the name of the Father and of the Son and of the Holy Spirit." Out of the Trinitarian formula of Baptism a three-part confession grew in Rome: "I believe in God the Father . . . and in Jesus Christ . . . and in the Holy Spirit." It was the original form of our Apostles' Creed. That the Christian faith is faith in the Father and the Son and the Holy Spirit was known by every Christian. But there was no pressing reason to think about the nature of the Holy Spirit. Who thinks about the air he breathes?

Even in Nicaea, when the great controversy about Christology was raging and the first decision regarding it was reached, the Holy Spirit was not felt to be a problem. The old Nicene Creed of 325 drew on earlier Eastern confessions, which derive finally from 1 Cor. 8:6. It confessed faith in one God, the Father and Creator, and in one Lord Jesus Christ. In its Christological article that creed develops a detailed doctrine of the relationship between the Father and the Son that reaches its climax in the *homoousios* ("being of one substance with the Father"). This received further clarification in the condemnations of the Arians which were appended. There is no "Third Article" such as in the old Roman baptismal confession. Following the "Second Article" there is only "and in the Holy Spirit." Not until the Niceno-Constantinopolitan Creed, the fuller creed of the Second Ecumenical Council in 381, is more said about the Holy Spirit. This is what appears as the "Nicene Creed" in our Confessions: "And in the Holy Spirit, the lord and giver of life, who proceeds from the Father . . . : who together with the Father and the Son is worshiped and glorified: who spoke by the prophets" [Tappert, p. 19].

Why was this expansion undertaken?What happened between the years 325 and 381? In the difficult struggles in 325 about the doctrine of the true deity of the Son it had become evident that the *homoousios* ("of one substance [with the Father]") of the Son is closely related to the *homoousios* of the Holy Spirit. One cannot confess that the Son is very God without also confessing that the Holy Spirit is very God and Lord.

This great recognition came to Athanasius as he struggled against the enemies of the *homoousios*, the Arians and the mediating theologians. This may have happened during his exile in the West. Here since Tertullian and Novatian there had been more engagement with the doctrine of the Holy Spirit, and the terms for the doctrine of the Trinity were already worked out. The Synod of Alexandria in 362 faced the false doctrine of the Pneumatomachi. They, along with the Arians, regarded the Holy Spirit as a creature. Athanasius opposed them and persuaded the synod to confess: "The Spirit is of the same essence and Godhead as the Father and the Son, and in the Trinity there is altogether nothing creaturely, nothing lower and nothing later" (Hefele, I, 728).

The other patriarchates were slow in accepting this. Basil the Great became a leading protagonist, while Gregory of Nazianzus, who presided at the Second Ecumenical Council in 381, gives evidence of a remarkable uncertainty in Oration 31, around the year 380:

> Some members of our own intelligentsia suppose the Holy Spirit to be an "activity," others a "creature"; others think of him as God; yet others fail to come to a decision, allegedly through reverence for the Scriptures, on the ground that they give no clear revelation on the question. The result is that they neither reverence the Spirit, nor dishonour him, but take up a kind of neutral position—or rather a pitiable position—with regard to him. Further, of those who suppose him divine, some are reverent towards him in thought, but no further; others go so far as to reverence him with their lips also. Others, even cleverer, I have heard measuring out the godhead: they admit that we have a union of three existences, but they put such a distance between them as to make the first unlimited in substance and power, the second unlimited in power, but not in substance, while the third they represent as circumscribed in both substance and power [Bettenson, *Later Christian Fathers*, p. 113].

Here we see the intensity of the theological struggle to confess the Holy Spirit. We may observe also that what was confessed by the council in 381 was not nearly so clear as what was confessed in 362 in Alexandria. The creed of 381, which we call the Nicene Creed, does not explicitly state the *homoousios* of the Holy Spirit; it is content to use expressions that imply it. But the church in the East as well as in the West has always taken these expressions as confessing the *homoousios* of the Holy Spirit. Since the Council of Constantinople in 381 the whole church has confessed that the Holy Spirit is God without reservation. And so the confession of the doctrine of the Holy Trinity was completed 300 years after the death of the apostles.

<h1 style="text-align:center">7</h1>

But was the doctrine of the Holy Trinity and with it the doctrine of the Holy Spirit really completed? Such was the conviction of the church. In reality, however, many questions remained open, as the subsequent history shows.

The East never went all the way in its confession of *homoousios*, for this means "of the same substance." So it was confessed by Athanasius and by the church in the West. The East, represented by the three great Cappadocians, Basil, Gregory of Nyssa, and Gregory of Nazianzus, could accept *homoousios* only in the sense of "similar substance." Athanasius permitted this as long as *homoios* or *homoiousios* ["similar" or "of similar substance"] was really understood in the sense of equality of being. Like every truly orthodox theologian, Athanasius was fighting for the doctrine, not for a theology. What mattered was the doctrine that God is One and that there are three Persons, whether the mystery of the Trinity was understood in the sense that the one God is Father, Son, and Holy Spirit, or in the sense that the three Persons, Father, Son, and Holy Spirit, are one God. Still today the mystery of the Trinity is confessed in the East as three in one (*Dreieinigkeit*) and in the West as one in three (*Dreifaltigkeit*). East and West complement each other in confessing that mystery which lies beyond the reach of comprehension. They belong together. In this way some echo of Origen was acceptable in the church of the East, and also in the West.

The East made no further advance, while the West went deeper with Augustine's probing of the doctrine of the Trinity. The church in the West gave the doctrine of the Trinity full confession in the *Symbolum Quicunque*, which came to be wrongly ascribed to Athanasius and was then called the Athanasian Creed, as it is in the Book of Concord. Here we have the confession of the doctrine which found its way into the Niceno-Constantinopolitan Creed with the *filioque*, which confesses that the Holy Spirit proceeds from the Father *and the Son*.

The Eastern Church subsequently pronounced this to be a falsification of the creed, and regarded this "falsification" of its most sacrosanct church text as a grievous sin of Rome. The papacy has always acknowledged that this creed can be used in the form employed by the Eastern Church because the addition does not contradict the original text. In the efforts toward reconciliation Rome has always required only that what is confessed with *filioque* should not be denied. This question of the *filioque* is the only creedal question between East and West, and therefore it has played a great, and often excessive, role in the polemics of the two confessions. Since Photius [ca. 820—891] Eastern theology has attempted to discover a great heresy in the *filioque*.

Yet this question is not one to hinder an eventual union of Rome with the Eastern Church. The difference in the way the doctrine is confessed lies along the lines of how the Trinity is understood, as indicated above. When the Eastern Church denies that the Spirit proceeds from the Son, there is a sense in which it continues to make room for the subordination of the Son to the Father which has its basis in Origen. But it is no more than a hint of Subordinationism, for Subordinationism itself is rejected by the *homoousios* of the Nicene Creed. And yet what was inherited from the great Origen has not quite disappeared. The situation might be put this way: As in many aspects of doctrine, cultus, and polity, the church of the East represents an older tradition. The church of the East did not participate in the development that took place in the West.

Why not? Here we come upon a problem which has not been sufficiently weighed in church history. It is the question of the consequences for the history of doctrine occasioned by the downfall of the ancient world.

8

When the Second Ecumenical Council met, the migration of nations had already begun. In the course of the next century the whole Western Empire fell to its Germanic conquerors. When the Third Ecumenical Council met in Ephesus in 431, Augustine was not there. He had died the previous year in Hippo Regius as it lay besieged by the Vandals. When the Fourth Ecumenical Council met in Chalcedon in October of 451, the Huns were at the doors of Italy.

Everyone knows how the history of doctrine fared in the East in the following generations under the influence of the disintegration of the empire, but no one can tell what was lost to the church in those centuries when the ancient civilization perished. How many questions were not pushed through to resolution simply for lack of thinkers with the competence to do so! We can only marvel that so much work, thought, and discussion was nevertheless accomplished. Under what deprivations, internal and external needs, did the later fathers have to work! Anastasius Sinaiticus in the seventh century indicates how hard it was to work in the wilderness, without a library, forced to rely on his memory for quotations. How the level of theological work sank in those centuries is clear if we compare Augustine with Gregory the Great.

The lamentable consequence of all this is that the doctrinal tasks of the ancient church were cut short. It was only centuries later that the heritage of Augustine was taken up by Western theology, and in the Eastern Church this never happened. So only in the West was the doctrine of the Trinity brought to what might be called completion. Of the doctrine of the Holy Spirit one has to say that also in the West it remained unfinished. The great creed of 381, our Nicene Creed, received remarkably little attention. At that time no one seemed to realize the importance of that synod in Constantinople with its meager 180 bishops. Its great achievement, the Niceno-Constantinopolitan Creed, appears first in the acts of the Council of Chalcedon, and only thereafter does it begin to supplant the creed of 325. The great ecumenical Niceno-Constantinopolitan Creed, which East and West have in common, and which they also share with the Nestorians and the Monophysites, has always had the character of an unfinished symphony.

The *filioque*, added in the West and condemned in the East as a creedal falsification, was not the only addition. In the Armenian liturgy at the place of the Third Article we read: "We believe in the Holy Spirit, who is not created and who is perfect. He has spoken in the law, in the prophets, and in the Gospels. At the Jordan he descended, he proclaimed his message to the apostles, and he dwells in the saints." In another version of the Armenian text the Holy Spirit is confessed as "of one being with the Father and the Son." (Caspari, *Quellen*, II, 33 [Hahn, p. 153].) One must not overlook the fact that such texts were not transmitted uniformly, as is shown by the variations in the different liturgies. The one just quoted is evidence of the tendency not to rest content with only an implicit confession of the *homoousios* of the Holy Spirit. This tendency came to fruition in the West in the full statement of the doctrine of the Trinity in the *Quicunque*.

9

"Who proceeds from the Father and the Son: who together with the Father and the Son is worshiped and glorified." The second "and the Son" (*et filio*) is already there in the creed of 381 and may be recognized as prompting the first "and the Son" (*filioque*). Already in the debates prior to 381 we find "who with the Father and the Son at the same time is worshiped and glorified." Placing the Holy Spirit on an equal level with the Father and the Son begins in the liturgy. Here is a classic case of the rule, so vital for understanding the history of doctrine, that the movement is from liturgy to doctrine (*Lex orandi lex credendi*). What comes to be confessed as doctrine in the church appears first in the liturgy. The doctrine of the Trinity appears first in the Trinitarian baptismal formula. "By grace alone" (*sola gratia*), proclaimed in the Reformation, was prayed in the Canon of the Mass. There in the prayer *Nobis quoque peccatoribus* the plea is made to God "not to reckon our merits but to pardon our transgressions" (*non aestimator meriti, sed veniae largitor*). *Sola gratia* was also sung in hymns of the Middle Ages: "King of majesty tremendous, Who dost free salvation send us . . . " ([*The Lutheran Hymnal* 607:8] *Rex tremendae majestatis, Qui salvandos salvas gratis*). So also the doctrine that the Holy Spirit is truly God, a Person of the Holy Trinity, appears first in the liturgy, when the Spirit is worshiped and glorified together with the Father and the Son. Adoration belongs only to God, to the Triune God or the Persons of the Holy Trinity. Whoever honors the Holy Spirit with the Father and the Son is confessing the Holy Spirit's full deity. Here arises an interesting problem. We observe that in the liturgy, in the church's solemn prayers or collects, the Holy Spirit is always named together with the Father and the Son. When the prayer is directed to the Father, it concludes: "through Jesus Christ Your Son, our Lord, who with You and the Holy Spirit lives and reigns to all eternity." When the prayer is directed to the Son, it concludes: "You who with the Father and the Holy Spirit live and reign to all eternity." But what about prayer to the Holy Spirit? Here we confront the remarkable fact that such prayers are never, or hardly ever, addressed to the Holy Spirit.

In the Eastern church they are unknown; only when the Triune God is called upon is the Holy Spirit also called upon. When I put this to an Eastern priest, he replied, "Well, you know that we do not have the *filioque*." To which I replied, "Yes, to be sure. Old Origen still remains a force to be reckoned with among you." And he agreed quite cheerfully.

Even in the Epiclesis, the solemn act in the liturgy, it is not the Holy Spirit that is called upon but the Father. The Father is called upon to send down the Spirit "upon us and the gifts here present" to make them the precious body and blood of Christ. We quote from the Epiclesis of the Liturgy of St. James, because here we have an especially full statement about the Holy Spirit:

> Send upon us and the gifts here present your all-holy Spirit, the Lord and giver of life, who with you, God the Father, and your only-begotten Son, is enthroned and rules together. He is of the same being (*homoousios*) and co-eternal. He has spoken in law and prophets and your new testament. He descended in the form of a dove upon our Lord Jesus Christ at the Jordan river and remained upon him. In the form of fiery tongues he came down upon the apostles in the upper room of the holy and glorious Zion on the day of the holy Pentecost. Him himself send, O Lord, your all-holy Spirit, upon us and these holy gifts here present . . . [Hanggi, p. 250; Jasper, p. 63].

It is impossible to make a more powerful confession of the Holy Spirit's true deity, and yet this church never took the step of calling upon the Holy Spirit Himself.

Also in the West it took centuries before this happened. Even today neither the Pentecost liturgy nor the Mass of the Holy Spirit contains such a prayer. There is only the call: "Come, Holy Spirit, fill the hearts of Your faithful, and kindle in them the fire of Your love," the *Veni, Sancte Spiritus*, which follows the Hallelujah or the Gradual and from which grew the medieval sequence and the hymn *Veni, Creator Spiritus* ["Come, Holy Ghost, Creator Blest]."

What is the explanation? Does this reticence perhaps have Biblical grounds? Holy Scripture has no calling upon the Holy Spirit comparable with the calling upon Christ that is found there. But when we consider the fact that in the Eastern liturgy (but not in the Roman Mass) a calling upon Mary has its settled place, we will scarcely be inclined to consider this a valid reason.

The puzzle grows when we consider that there was indeed a church in whose liturgy prayers were addressed to the Holy Spirit, the Visigothic church in Spain. In its liturgy, called the Mozarabic liturgy, we find: "O Holy Spirit, who proceeds from the Father and the Son (*qui a Patre Filioque procedis*), teach us to do the truth, so that You, who have undertaken procession from the Father and the Son, may with love invisible join us to them from whom You so ineffably proceed" (*MPL*, 86, 691). This is only one example from the *Breviarium Gothicum*. In Isidore's *Missale Mixtum* the Holy Spirit is called upon in the Postpridie to accept the sacrifice: "Accept, we pray, O Holy Spirit, omnipotent God, the sacrifices . . . For you are in truth that fire which divinely accepted and consumed the sacrifices of our fathers. . . ." Then before the Our Father the Holy Spirit is called upon anew: "O Paraclete, Spirit, You who continue to be with the Father and the Son one God in Trinity, so fill our minds that with You praying for us we may here on earth with great confidence say, 'Our Father . . .' " (*MPL* 85, 620 [Beckmann, *Quellen*, pp. 95 f.].)

Clearly these prayers grew out of Augustine's doctrine of the Trinity. They follow logically from the *filioque*, whose grounds were stated by Augustine and which was included in the creed as confessed in the Visigothic church in Spain (Toledo 589), from where it traveled to the kingdom of the Franks. The history that led to this development is unknown to us. It happened during the dark period of the migration of the nations which followed the death of Augustine. The prayers of the Mozarabic liturgy are what is left to us as monuments from a forgotten period of the church's history, a period when from the orthodox doctrine of the Trinity, as Augustine had completed it for the West, the conclusion was drawn that in the prayers of the liturgy the church not only may but must pray to the Third Person of the Trinity, the Holy Spirit who proceeds from the Father and the Son, who with the Father and the Son is of one being, true God from eternity to eternity.

That this liturgical development did not spread more widely through the church in the West may be explained by the fact that Rome was not aware of this calling upon the Spirit in church that was customary in Spain. Rome preserved an older type of dealing with the Trinity in the liturgy. It did not allow the liturgical consequences of the *filioque* doctrine to come to expression. This seems to explain why most Roman Catholic liturgiologists in their debates about whether and where there may be traces of an Epiclesis in the Mass have tended to overlook the fact that the Mass contains a calling upon the Holy Spirit in a way which is more than the Eastern church's calling upon the Father to send the Spirit. It is there in the Offertory prayer: "Come, Sanctifier, almighty, eternal God, and bless this sacrifice" (*Veni sanctificator omnipotens aeterne Deus, et benedic hoc sacrificium*). *Sanctificator*, the One who sanctifies, is a designation of the Holy Spirit. That this is so is evidenced by the Mozarabic liturgy, where in the same prayer the Spirit is explicitly named.

The characteristic conservatism of the liturgy is perhaps explanation enough for the prayers to the Holy Spirit not being further developed. The liturgy reaches back into the time when there was as yet no Trinitarian dogma. In the Gloria in Excelsis, for example, the Holy Spirit receives only bare mention at the end, as is also the case in the creed of 325. In the Middle Ages hymns were sung to the Holy Spirit, and the churches of the Reformation have the usage of prayers to the Holy Spirit. That there is nothing here conflicting with Roman doctrine is evidenced by the solemn prayer with which the sessions of the Vatican Council were begun. We quote a few words from the lengthy prayer addressed to the Holy Spirit: "We are here, Lord, Holy Spirit. We stand here before You held back by the greatness of our sins, but it is in Your name that we are especially assembled. Come to us and be with us. . . . As You work our judgments be also their Health, You who alone with the Father and His Son possess the glorious name. . . ." Then come further prayers, among which there is an indirect prayer for the Spirit: "We beseech You, O Lord, that the Paraclete, who proceeds from You, may enlighten our souls and lead us into all truth, as Your Son has promised, who with You lives . . ."

No, there is simply nothing that can be raised as an objection to our praying to the Holy Spirit just as we do to the Father and the Son. Is our neglect of such prayer perhaps the reason why Christianity has erred into so many false pathways? Has the place left empty of prayers to the Holy Spirit perhaps been occupied by the cult of the saints? Has Mary perhaps in practice often come to occupy the place that belongs to the Holy Spirit? And what has become of the Trinity when a pope in our day died with the prayer: "Jesus, Mary, Joseph, into your hands I commend my spirit"? And of the churches which claim to have the heritage of the Reformation, must we not also say that they, even though in different ways, show loss of the true faith in the Holy Spirit?

10

The doctrine of the Holy Spirit belongs to the uncompleted doctrines of the church. Can we find the explanation for this in the fact that, strictly speaking, the doctrine of the Holy Spirit belongs with *eschatology*, the doctrine of the Last Things? When on the day of Pentecost the Holy Spirit was poured out upon the apostles, there was fulfilled, as Peter said in the church's first Pentecost sermon, that which according to the prophet Joel was to happen "in the last days," in the days of the Messiah, at the end of the world. The Third Article of the creed indeed has to do with the Last Things, with what will happen at the end of the world. The Holy Spirit as the possession of the entire people of God, not merely as an occasional and temporary gift, is a gift of the end time.

The Holy Spirit brings blessed eternity into time now in this world, forgiveness of sins, life and salvation. So also the one holy catholic and apostolic church which we confess in this same article is a fact of the end time. The church, God's own holy people, makes its journey from one age to the next, traveling through the wilderness of this world. It has been delivered from the slavery of Egypt, the old age, but has not yet arrived in the land of promise, the new age. To this article belongs faith in the resurrection of the dead and the waiting for the life of the world to come. This article ends in eternity. Therefore it necessarily remains uncompleted.

It has often been supposed that the neglect of the doctrine of the Holy Spirit is to be explained by the fact that here we are confronted with things intangible. There is more than a grain of truth in this. However, we ought never to forget the actuality of what the Holy Spirit does. What the church of the apostles and of the early Christians experienced as the reality of the Holy Spirit was not first of all the spectacular gifts of the Spirit which occurred at that time, the gifts of healing, prophecy, speaking in tongues, and whatever else has in the church's history been regarded as extraordinarily miraculous manifestations of the Spirit. Far more important were the great and lasting workings of faith, hope, and love.

If one reads the old sermons and records of what the ancient church experienced every year in the time between Easter and Pentecost, an echo of which can still be heard in the old liturgical texts, then one can say that what was experienced at this time of the church year was an inexpressible joy. We spoke of this in an earlier letter [No. 37, *Freudenzeit der Kirche*]). This joy lives in our Lord's Farewell Discourses, which have been the source of so many Gospel readings in the time from Easter to Pentecost. It is the more-than- earthly joy that we hear from the mouths of the ancient martyrs, the joy that is a foretaste of everlasting blessedness. It was not just due to a misunderstanding of the word "Paraclete" that He came to be called the Comforter. "You have sorrow now, but I will see you again and your hearts will rejoice, and no one will take your joy from you" [John 16:22]. "Your sorrow will turn into joy" [v. 20]. " . . . that My joy may be in you, and that your joy may be full"[John 15:11]. All of this is in what our Lord promises of the Holy Spirit, the Comforter.

One of the deepest heartaches of human existence is the riddle of work cut short, left unfinished. Many of our Lutheran churches have in this century twice lost the fairest flowering of their young theologians.

We who were the teachers of one of these lost generations have often asked ourselves what sense there could be in such a tragedy. There is no other answer than faith in the Holy Spirit, He who brings uncompleted work to completion. We remember those nuns in the French Revolution who, as they were lead from their cloister to the scaffold, sang the *Veni, Creator Spiritus*. They stood in the great apostolic succession of the confessors and martyrs of all times, down to those in our own day. Somewhere in China faith in the Lord Christ is sealed with the death of nameless martyrs. No one will know their confession—one of the meanings of *confessio* is the grave of a martyr—until that day when all graves will be opened.

Our Lord, after His Farewell Discourses, prayed His High Priestly Prayer thinking of all His faithful ones, also those known only to Him. In this prayer He speaks words which no man ever prayed in the face of death, in the face of what, to all human evaluation, marked His life and work as uncompleted: "Father, the hour has come; glorify Thy Son that the Son may glorify Thee. . . . I glorified Thee on earth, having accomplished the work which Thou gavest Me to do. . . . I have manifested Thy name . . . " [John 17:1, 4, 6]

"I have glorified *You*. I have done the work *You* gave me to do. I have made *Your* name known to men." Where the church, where we servants of the Lord, can speak thus as we follow Jesus on the way of the cross: "We have glorified *You* and not ourselves; we have done the work *You* gave us to do, not what we have sought for ourselves; we have manifested *Your* name, not our name or the name of our big or little church"—only insofar as we can say this will there be a fulfillment of the promise: "I will pray the Father, and He will give you another Counselor ["Comforter" in the German] to be with you forever, even the Spirit of truth, whom the world cannot receive, because it neither sees Him nor knows Him; you know Him, for He dwells with you, and will be in you" [John 14:16–17]. Where this is a vital reality in the church, there the doctrine of the Holy Spirit is no longer an abstract dogma, for then the Holy Spirit is a living Reality. The world will never understand this; also not the world that is in the church, also not the world that is in our own hearts. But He who has overcome the world, also the world in the church and the world in our stubborn and despairing hearts, says to all who believe in His name: "The Spirit of truth . . . dwells with you, and will be in you."

We hardly need to say any more about what this faith in the Holy Spirit means for the church today and for us pastors. Without this faith the history of the church and the life of Christians would have no meaning. But where this faith is alive and truly taught, there is the one holy catholic and apostolic church, to which the promise has been given that the gates of hell shall not prevail against it.

Dear brother pastors, let us pray for this faith, and in this faith do the work given us to do for Christ's church.

ARTICLE VII OF THE AUGSBURG CONFESSION IN THE PRESENT CRISIS OF LUTHERANISM

Letters to Lutheran Pastors, No. 53
April 1961

On July 1, 1868, there was the first meeting, in Hannover, of the General Evangelical-Lutheran Conference. The meeting began with divine service in St. Mark's Church. The preacher was Luthardt, who became editor of their church paper. The text was 1 Cor. 4:1 f.; the theme, "Of the True Faithfulness of the Servants of Jesus Christ." Harless from Munich opened the sessions with an address through which there rang a deep tone of repentance. He spoke of the common plight of Lutheranism. "If we speak of our wounds and what we suffer from them, we do not speak so much of wounds which others have given us, but of the wounds which we have inflicted upon ourselves in ignorance or unfaithfulness." Then came the hymn "Lord Jesus Christ, with us abide, For round us falls the eventide." Then Kliefoth from Schwerin gave his famous address: "What Is Required of Church Government in the Lutheran Church According to Article VII of the Augsburg Confession?"

If we only had more time to attend this meeting and listen to these great men! We are in desperate need of knowing our history through the last century and a half. The accounts given in the usual textbooks show little understanding or sympathy for what happened; in some there is little more than shreds and falsification.

But we want to point out that in one of Lutheranism's most dire crises Article VII of the Augsburg Confession came to occupy the center of the discussion. What was at stake was nothing more and nothing less than the existence of the Lutheran territorial churches in Germany as

Lutheran. In the wars of 1864 and 1866 Prussia had annexed Schleswig-Holstein, Hannover, and Electoral Hesse. This brought the demand that the Prussian Union should be imposed also on these new provinces of the Prussian state. Nothing characterizes the situation better than the famous letter which Harless, the president of the Lutheran Conference, wrote to Bismarck in November of 1870. At the same time Bishop Ketteler of Mainz, the spokesman for the Catholic bishops in Germany, wrote a similar letter to the chancellor. Their plea that in the constitution, which was being prepared for the new German Empire, the rights of the churches in Germany should be respected, was in vain. (Documents in Th. Heckel's *Adolph von Harless*, pp. 482 ff.) Harless spoke of the profound concern of committed Lutherans in Germany that the Lutheran Church would be robbed of its place in territory after territory, with the result that it could only continue to exist in small free churches, or that Lutheranism would become only a theological viewpoint within other, non-Lutheran churches. "Only with the profoundest grief can one think such thoughts through to the end, that the Lutheran Church . . . would have her lamp cast aside in Germany" (p. 485).

In this situation the Lutherans pondered Article VII of the Augsburg Confession. It was too late. Today, after almost a century, Harless's prophecy has been fulfilled in Germany. Apart from the free churches, Lutheranism no longer lives on as a church but as a viewpoint, as a "theological school of thought," within one Evangelical Church, as both Schleiermacher and Barth said. Even the territorial churches which are nominally and *de iure* Lutheran have no longer *de facto* preserved the Lutheran confessional position.

The men of 1868 turned their eyes to Lutheranism elsewhere in the world, to the Scandinavian lands and to America. Just at that time in America the gathering together of confessional Lutherans was under way. The General Council was gathering the confessional synods which could no longer go along with the unionistic General Synod. In the Midwest, confessional synods were joining with Missouri to form the Synodical Conference (1872). At that time the first beginnings of ecumenical Lutheranism could be noticed everywhere. The question as to what creates church fellowship according to Scripture and the Confessions was always the thing that caused separations and led to new unions. A new day was dawning for the Lutheran Church.

Today the question we cannot escape is whether the way things went with Lutheranism in Germany will be the way things go with

41

Lutheranism elsewhere in the world. Will Lutheranism everywhere become merely a viewpoint within church bodies that are not in fact Lutheran? The confessionally committed Lutherans in Denmark, Norway, and Sweden are even more lonely today than their brethren in the faith in Germany. The churches to which they belong are now only nominally Lutheran. Things are moving in the same direction also in America, and with the same speed with which everything seems to happen in the New World. The fact that Lutheranism now faces the greatest crisis in its history cannot be hidden by the putting together of big new church bodies in America, nor by the gigantic organization of the Lutheran World Federation with its reported 60 million "Lutherans," including the atheists and Communists in whole countries that once embraced the Reformation. The crisis is evidenced theologically in the general uncertainty regarding the great article of the Augsburg Confession about the church. Whatever else it may mean, this article is the Magna Charta of the Lutheran Church. We will all do well to study it thoroughly, so that we will be up to the tasks which lie before each of us.

1

Article VII of the Augsburg Confession is the first doctrinal statement ever made in Christendom about what the church is and wherein is her unity. Before the Reformation, people were content to confess the statement of faith in the Nicene Creed: "I believe (the Greek text adds 'in') one holy, catholic, and apostolic church." What this church is and wherein lies its unity, holiness, catholicity, and apostolicity— these were questions which theologians wrote about, and which were variously thought of by the various Christian denominations in ancient times, such as the Montanists, Novatians, Donatists, and Catholics. For the word "catholic," when used as in Catholic Church (Augustine, *communio catholica*), referred to only one of the numerous groups which regarded themselves as the true church. Yet they did not feel it was necessary to have a doctrinal definition of what the church is, not even in the Catholic Church or churches (they were not always in church fellowship with each other).

Many of those who participated in the World Conference on Faith and Order in Lausanne in 1927 were astonished to hear the representative of the Ecumenical Patriarch declare at the beginning that the question "What is the church?" belongs to the open questions which theologians are free to have their disputes about. Only that is church dogma which is stated in the Third Article of the Nicene Creed. Similarly Rome. The Roman Catechism speaks of the church in its exposition of the creed, but the catechism is not dogma. So we find lively debate in the 19th century about what the church is, particularly in German Catholicism since Möhler. We cannot here speak of how the Vatican Council of 1869/70 in vain sought to complete a dogma "Of the Church of Christ" but had to leave this task to the future. All previous documents, such as the encyclical *Mystici corporis*, can only be viewed as preparatory.

Echoes of Article VII of the Augsburg Confession are to be found in all the Reformed confessions of the 16th century. Of particular significance is Article 19 of the Anglican Thirty-Nine Articles, where the definition according to the official English text reads:

> The visible church of Christ is a congregation of faithful men (Latin *coetus fidelium*), in which the pure Word of God is preached, and the Sacraments be duly administered according to Christ's ordinance in all those things that of necessity are requisite to the same.

The reason why the Augsburg Confession had to speak on this matter is clear. The article goes back to Article 12 of the Schwabach Articles, and behind that lies Luther's *Great Confession* of 1528:

> Next, I believe that there is one holy Christian ("Christian" is used here, as in the late Middle Ages, for *catholica* in the sense of embracing all of Christendom) Church on earth, i.e., the community or number or assembly of all Christians in all the world, the one bride of Christ, and his spiritual body of which he is the only head. The bishops or priests are not her heads or lords or bridegrooms, but servants, friends, and—as the word "bishop" implies— superintendents, guardians, or stewards.
>
> This Christian Church exists not only in the realm of the Roman Church or pope, but in all the world, as the prophets foretold that the gospel of Christ would spread throughout the world, Psalm 2 [:8], Psalm 19 [:4]. Thus this Christian Church is physically dispersed among pope, Turks, Persians, Tartars, but spiritually gathered in one gospel and faith, under one head, i.e., Jesus Christ. For the papacy is assuredly the true realm of Antichrist, the real anti-Christian tyrant, who sits in the temple of God and rules with human commandments, as Christ in Matthew 24 [:24] and Paul in II Thessalonians 2 [:3 f.] declare; although the Turk and all heresies, wherever they may be, are also included in this abomination which according to prophecy will stand in the holy place, but are not to be compared to the papacy (WA 26, 506 f. [American Edition 37, 367 f.]).

43

Even if we were to disregard the doctrine of the Antichrist, which was for Luther a part of the doctrine of the church, this quotation shows why the Reformation had to ask and answer the question: "What is the church?" The highest office in the church had rejected the holy Gospel, and those who proclaimed this Gospel had been put out of the fellowship of the church. For this reason Luther and those with him had to say why they could not recognize the papal excommunication as exclusion from the church. Thus the ecclesiological question was put, and an answer had to be given.

2

The answer which Article VII of the Augsburg Confession gives to the question of the church is best understood within its context. What it says is supplemented particularly in Articles V, VIII, and XXVIII. The whole of the Augsburg Confession is the context for Article VII, and its great exposition is given in the Apology. This does not mean that our Confessions say everything there is to be said about the church and leave no question open. They do not claim to do this.

The doctrine of the church is like other parts of Christian doctrine, both simple and inexhaustible. "A seven-year-old child," says Luther, "knows what the church is, namely, holy believers and sheep who hear the voice of their shepherd" (Smalcald Articles III, XII, 2). While a child may well know the voice of its Good Shepherd and yet the deepest thinkers through the centuries of the church have not been able to exhaust the truth of Scripture regarding the Lord Christ, so also the actuality of the church remains an inexhaustible problem for theology. There are questions which our Confessions do not answer, nor have they been answered by other churches.

One such question has to do with how it is to be understood when the New Testament speaks of the church as the body of Christ. In what sense is it a body, according to Scripture? Certainly not in the sense in which the word "body" is used of a number of people joined together in an association. Not only what we call the universal church is the body of Christ, but also "the church of God in Corinth" or in any other place. What is the relationship between the "sacramental" and the "spiritual" body of Christ?

Another question which did not engage our fathers in the 16th century is the eschatological sense of the church. There is church only in the end time. "In the last days" the prophecy of Joel was fulfilled at

Pentecost (Acts 2:16–21). John says in his day, "It is the last hour" (1 John 2:18).

For answering such questions our Confessions provide vital resources, as for example in the doctrine of the Antichrist. But unfolding them demands deep study of Scripture. In this sense Vilmar was right in speaking of the doctrine of the church as an uncompleted doctrine. There are depths not yet plumbed to which the church may be led. Throughout the whole of Christianity questions are today being asked about the church, and so also among the Lutherans around the world. Our church would be dead if we supposed that we had nothing more to learn.

3

What is the church? Our Confession gives an answer which in a noteworthy way immediately differentiates itself from the answers of other churches. Article 19 of the Anglican Thirty-Nine Articles reproduces the definition of Article VII, but makes a characteristic change by inserting "visible." "The *visible* Church of Christ is the congregation . . . " This is done in opposition to the confessions of all the other Reformed churches. These, guided by Zwingli, Bucer, and Calvin, regard the true church as invisible. The Anglican insertion was perhaps done in deliberate opposition to the Scottish Confession of 1560, which links the doctrine of the church with the doctrine of the Holy Trinity and the doctrine of the person of Christ, and then says: "This Kirk is invisible, known only to God, who alone knows whom He has chosen" [16, Cochrane, p. 175].

Our Confession does not make this distinction between an invisible and a visible church. Luther does indeed, now and then, speak of the church as invisible, but in an altogether different sense. It would have been better for Lutheran theology never to have spoken as though there were two churches, one visible and another invisible. This distinction derives from the Reformed doctrine of predestination. It goes back to Augustine, and in the Middle Ages is found in Wycliffe. The invisible church is made up of all the predestined, the visible church of the baptized. It is possible to be a member of the one without being a member of the other. The sacrament of Baptism is here then only the outward sign of the baptism with the Holy Spirit. For the person who is not predestined to eternal life the baptism with water remains only a sign without effect.

45

This distinction is rejected by the Lutheran Church as unbiblical. Baptism according to the New Testament is not only a sign but the means that washes away sins (Eph. 5:26), "the washing of regeneration" (Titus 3:5). So there are not two churches, one the visible fellowship of those who have received a sign of regeneration, and the other the invisible fellowship of those who have been born again of the Holy Spirit to eternal life. Our church also confesses election to eternal life and knows that those baptized may be lost, and that by their own fault. We bow before the God whose hidden decisions, which He has not revealed to us, we do not understand. We bow before the God who "desires all men to be saved and to come to the knowledge of the truth" [1 Tim. 2:4], and who yet allows so many to be lost eternally. But we can never surrender the promises that are bound up with the means of grace. We can never say that He did not mean His promises. A person can lose the blessing of Baptism by not again and again, yes daily, receiving the promise of Christ in faith. But the promise remains. Baptism remains the same.

In the controversies about Baptism between the Lutherans and the Reformed in the 16th century, which we should study far more thoroughly, our theologians liked to refer to the "one Baptism" of Eph. 4:5, which was also taken into the Nicene Creed. From this great Pauline passage, on which also Article VII of the Augsburg Confession rests, as also from the "one God . . . and one Lord" in 1 Cor. 8:6, we have the repeated "one" in the Nicene Creed: "I believe in *one* God, the Father . . . and in *one* Lord Jesus Christ . . . *one* holy, catholic, and apostolic church . . . *one* Baptism for the remission of sins." What is confessed here from the New Testament, "one Baptism," is a defense not only against the idea that Baptism can be repeated, but also against the Platonizing splitting up of this sacrament into a physical baptism and a spiritual baptism.

This is true not only of the means of grace, but also of the church. Our Confession confesses only one church, and not two. The church may not be split into an invisible one and a visible one, no matter what some later Lutheran theologians may have thought about it. Thereby our Confession follows the Nicene and the Apostles' Creed, and the New Testament. When the question is put whether Article VII of the Augsburg Confession is speaking of the invisible church, as the Reformed understood this article, or of the visible church, as the Anglicans interpreted it for themselves, we simply have to say that the question is

46

wrongly put; the article does not know this distinction, and neither does the New Testament.

4

This great article has been taken apart in some unhelpful attempts to explain it. The first sentence is said to refer to the invisible church, since the one holy church, the one that goes on forever, is an article of faith and therefore is invisible. The second sentence, on the other hand, is taken as referring to the visible church, since the congregation of all believers, in which the Gospel is preached and the sacraments are bestowed, is made up of visible people among whom here on earth the means of grace are administered and received.

The contradictions inherent in this should have led to the realization that the question is wrongly put. The author of the Augsburg Confession was not one who was unable to think clearly and logically. Neither was Luther, for that matter, who shared responsibility for the Schwabach Articles and expressed the matter in the same way in his "Great Confession" of 1528. Can one imagine that they would not have noticed such a confusion of concepts? If we examine the debates over Article VII in the 19th and 20th centuries, we find that these controversies about its meaning do not derive from any unclarity in the Confession, but rather from the unclear thinking of its interpreters, who attempted to read into it later theological notions and the categories of their own ecclesiology.

Like other articles, so also this one basically sets down the teaching of the New Testament, where the church is always both an actual, concrete gathering of people whom one can see, and also the communion of saints, the people of God, the body of Christ which one must believe. What the Jews and the heathen saw in Corinth was a group of people who assembled together. What they did not see was the holiness of these people, was the character of this group as the people of God, the body of Christ, the temple of the Holy Spirit. Yes, also the saints in Corinth, to the extent that they were really saints and not Pharisees or hypocrites, did not themselves see the holiness that was theirs.

That your sins are forgiven must be believed. The Christians in Corinth had to believe that they were God's people and that in, with, and under their visible assembly the spiritual body of Christ was present—just as they could not see, taste, or feel that the consecrated bread and the consecrated wine in the Lord's Supper were the true body and the true blood of Christ. They had to believe that.

Also for the church of the New Testament the church was not an article of sight but an article of faith in the strict sense of the word. And so it was in the church which confessed the Nicene Creed and therein the great article of the one, holy church. Only in faith could the Catholics in ancient Christendom (already then Catholic was a confessional designation) assert that they were the true church and not the Novatians, who asserted the same regarding themselves, for they not only held the orthodox faith but also had the older forms of church discipline. Only in faith could Augustine know that not the Donatists were the true church, but rather that fellowship which he called the *communio catholica*. The church is always an object of faith.

This is basically the case also for Roman Catholicism today. The conviction that the church is and must be as visible as was the ancient people of Israel, as is any social organization of people on earth, is qualified by the fact that Rome never knows exactly where the boundaries of the church are. In what sense can those who are excommunicated be said to be members of the church, whose members they remain? When schismatic churches possess the priesthood and episcopal consecrations, when even the baptisms performed by heretics, if they are done properly, are valid, and when today heretics are called "separated brethren," where is then the exact boundary of the church? Already Optatus of Mileve [fourth century] bestowed the name of brother upon the Donatists, with exhaustive theological grounds for doing so in his seven books on the Donatist schism (Migne, *PL* 11, 962 ff., 1029 f.). The editors of the German edition of Thomas [Aquinas] speak in the introduction to Vol. 29 of "the visible church of Christ, which is visible only in and through its sacraments." Do we not here have the Catholic counterpart to the Lutheran doctrine of the means of grace, the Gospel and the sacraments as the *notae ecclesiae*, the only marks by which we can in faith recognize the presence of the church?

Basically it is the conviction of all Christianity that the church is an article of faith and so not an object of observation. Otherwise the article of faith confessed in the creed about the church would have no sense. "It is necessary that everything which is believed should be hidden," says Luther in *De servo arbitrio* (*opus est, ut omnia quae creduntur, abscondantur*, WA 18, 633 [American Edition 33, 62]).When he then draws the conclusion: "The Church is hidden, the saints are unknown" (*Abscondita est ecclesia, latent sancti* [WA 18, 652; American Edition 33, 89]), the Catholics have never acknowledged this. They must admit, however, that there is some truth here. That is shown by the quotation we have cited about the sacraments. Even for Rome the church is not quite so visible as the kingdom of France or the republic of Venice, as Bellarmine once maintained in his extreme polemics against the Reformation [Mirbt, p. 361].

5

One great truth, then, that is confessed in Article VII of the Augsburg Confession is that the church of Christ is always an object of faith. The other great truth is that it is always a reality in this world. It is made up of living people. So the Apology protests against the misunderstanding which thinks of the church as a "Platonic state":

> We are not dreaming about some Platonic republic, as has been slanderously alleged, but we teach that this church actually exists, made up of true believers and righteous men scattered throughout the world. And we add its marks, the pure teaching of the Gospel and the sacraments. This church is properly called"the pillar of truth" (I Tim. 3:15), for it retains the pure Gospel and what Paul calls the "foundation" (I Cor 3:12) . . . (Apology VII and VIII, 20 [Tappert p. 171]).

In order to grasp what our Confession teaches about the reality of the church in the world, one must learn to grasp what kind of realities the Gospel and the sacraments are for Luther and for the Lutheran Church of the Reformation. Modern man, like the educated humanistic people at that time, sees in the Gospel a religious message, the proclamation of the truths of Christendom. He understands the sacraments as holy actions which symbolically represent a deeper truth. By the power that inheres in a symbol they could be more than mere signs.

Luther goes back to Holy Scripture. There the Word of God is more than a religious message. "Behold, I have put My words in your mouth. See, I have set you this day over nations and over kingdoms, to pluck up and to break down, to destroy and to overthrow, to build and to plant" (Jer. 1:9–10). Thus the Lord speaks to Jeremiah in the hour of his call, and similarly He speaks to all His prophets. Man's word can do much, but it cannot do what God's Word can do, the Word of the Creator and Redeemer, the Word of the Judge and the Fulfiller. Therefore God's own Word has been put into the mouth of His prophets. This Word has not only created the world but also makes history. The fate of Israel as well as of the Eastern peoples and world empires is determined through this Word. "But now thus says the Lord, He who created you, O Jacob, He who formed you, O Israel: 'Fear not, for I have redeemed you. . . .

I give Egypt as your ransom. Ethiopia and Seba in exchange for you" (Is. 43:1, 3). "Thus says the Lord to His anointed, to Cyrus, whose right hand I have grasped, to subdue nations before him and ungird the loins of kings, to open doors before him that gates may not be closed. I will go before you . . . " (Is. 45:1–2). This is not just interpretation of history. This is a revelation of the deepest core of the world-historical events of that time, when the Neobabylonian Empire collapsed under Persian attack and Israel was saved. God's Word makes history.

That is also true of the Word of God committed to the church. Also the fates of the peoples of modern Europe are determined by the Word of God which is proclaimed to them, is believed and rejected. When in the empty churches of modern nations the Word of God is preached by a faithful pastor to a handful of people, then this Word, because it is God's Word, becomes a judgment upon people who have rejected God and the faith of their fathers. And at the same time it becomes the Word of deliverance for the "holy remnant."

In my first years in the pastoral office in the environs of Berlin we pastors often asked what would become of the villages in which, Sunday after Sunday, divine service was held with a few old women—that is, if the service was not canceled. Kliefoth often asked what might come upon Mecklenburg, where the landed gentry refused to give their day laborers Saturday afternoon off, with the result that all the work that they had to do for themselves had to be done on Sunday. Today we know how such contempt for God's Word is punished. "For the Word of God is living and active, sharper than any two-edged sword" (Heb. 4:12). That is so today, as it has been for thousands of years, and will be so also in the future until the end of the world. The recognition of this reality of the Word of God is the basis for recognizing the reality of the church.

It is perhaps even more difficult for modern man to recognize the reality of the Word when it comes to him as Gospel. The reality of God's judgment is still to some extent recognizable. But the reality of grace is impenetrable to modern man, because in losing an understanding for sin he has also lost an understanding for grace. This is evidenced by the decline of confession and absolution in Protestantism—which, by the way (something we should not forget), has its parallels in the Roman church. What does it mean to go to Confession once a year, or not for many years and then on the deathbed, for the unchurched masses of nominal Catholics in Vienna, Paris, or Rio de Janeiro? Do *we* still know the solid joy of being sure that the absolution I have received from my

50

pastor is God's forgiveness, spoken by the mouth of His servant, and therefore valid in heaven? The heart of the Gospel is the forgiveness of sins—not a doctrine about it, that and how there is forgiveness, but the bestowing of this forgiveness in the absolution. The same is to be said also of the sacraments of Baptism and the Lord's Supper. Do we still believe what actually happens in these sacraments as we learned it in the Catechism?

Only when we again grasp the reality of the Word of God and the sacraments will we also grasp the reality of the church as confessed in our Confessions. The church is no Platonic state, but an actuality in the world. It is "the assembly of all believers among whom the Gospel is preached in its purity and the holy sacraments are administered according to the Gospel" (Article VII, German text). The administration of the means of grace happens here in this world. They are extended to people who are all quite tangible. As the Lord is active in, with, and under the dealings of men—as He baptizes, absolves, consecrates, gives His true body and His true blood, gives the Holy Spirit, faith, life, blessing—so a holy church is present in, with, and under the assembly of these concrete human beings. For the promise of God bound up with these means remains valid under all circumstances.

From this it is clear that the first and second sentences of the article are indissolubly bonded together. The one church of faith, spoken of in the first sentence, is identical with the visible assembly insofar as this church is present in, with, and under this assembly. This does not exclude the fact that there may be among them hypocrites and unbelievers, unworthy and hypocritical pastors. These belong outwardly to the church as "an association of outward ties and rites" (*societas externarum rerum ac rituum*). But hidden in this external assembly is "an association of faith and of the Holy Spirit in men's hearts" (*societas fidei et Spiritus Sancti in cordibus*), "the inward communion of eternal blessings in the heart, as of the Holy Ghost, of faith, of the fear and love of God," as the German translation by J. Jonas reproduces the Latin text of the Apology (VII and VIII, 5 [final quotation from *Concordia Triglotta*, p. 227]).

There are, then, not two churches but the one church, which the eyes of man see as a congregation or church body, but in which the eyes of God see those who actually and truly belong to the church—perhaps only a small group—and are not just "mingled" (*admixti*, AC VIII) with it. That is the church *proprie dicta*, the church in the real sense, in contrast with the church *large dicta*,) the church in the broader sense.

51

It is, however, always the one church that is spoken of, whether in the strict or the wider sense. God's all-knowing eye recognizes in it the "association of faith and of the Holy Spirit in men's hearts." Our human eyes see only the "association of outward ties and rites," but in faith in the Lord and His promises we know that wherever the means of grace are, there Christ has His church.

6

What is confessed of the church in the Lutheran Confessions, that the church is something believed and confessed and not something of our observation, and that the church is a reality in the world, is basic for what Article VII says of the *unity* of the church. As with the church, so also with the unity of the church: It is an object of faith. As no one can see the body of Christ, so also no one can see its unity. If we were to suppose that the whole of Christianity was united in a globe-encircling organization, on the basis of a constitution and cultus acknowledged by all, and even if the same could be said of all doctrine, this union would not yet make the *Una Sancta* visible. Even in such an "ecumenical church," which many today hold up as the ideal, there would be those who belong to it only externally and are not members of the body of Christ. Even in such a giant church, including everyone who claims to be a Christian, the *Una Sancta* would yet be hidden. It would be just the same as with any local congregation.

Paul calls the Christians in Corinth "those sanctified in Christ Jesus, called to be saints." He speaks of that congregation as "the church of God which is at Corinth" [1 Cor. 1:2]. These are statements of faith. In faith he knows that God's church, the one body of Christ, is there in that pile of sinners. They are threatening to destroy the communion of the church, the unity of the body of Christ, with their party strife, these semi-believers who are so proud of their knowledge (Gnosis) and do not even know what the Lord's Supper is and even doubt the resurrection of the dead. Without contradicting himself Paul can write to this congregation, in which there is so much for him to reproach: "I give thanks to God always for you because of the grace of God which was given you in Christ Jesus, that in every way you were enriched in Him with all speech and all knowledge—even as the testimony to Christ was confirmed among you." Because the preaching of Christ is there, and has created faith, therefore Paul is certain that he who has called them will surely sustain them to the end (1 Cor. 1:4 ff.). The same is the case with the original church in Jerusalem. Acts speaks of that congregation as being "of one heart and soul," and then with striking honesty goes on to tell of Ananias and Sapphira, who lied to God, and then of the first dispute in the church, a dispute about money [Acts 4:32; 5:1–11; 6:1].

Even where we experience Christian, brotherly fellowship, "heart and heart together united," there too the communion of saints remains an article of faith, for this communion, the *koinōnia* of which the New Testament speaks, is a work of the Holy Spirit. It not only binds the believers together, but it also unites us "with the Father and with His Son Jesus Christ" (1 John 1:3). The mystery of this communion reaches into the communion within the Holy Trinity. "The glory which Thou hast given Me I have given to them, that they may be one even as We are one, I in them and Thou in Me, that they may become perfectly one" (John 17:22–23).

This unity is always an object of faith, not of observation, even though the world may see something of its working: "Behold, how they love one another." The Apology describes the *Una Sancta* with these words: " . . . men scattered throughout the world who agree on the Gospel and have the same Christ, the same Holy Spirit, and the same sacraments, whether they have the same human traditions or not" [Articles VII and VIII, 10; Tappert, p. 170]. [Ed. note: Dr. Sasse quotes both the German and Latin texts, but they are quite similar.] Hidden under the various church bodies with their different languages and nationalities, constitutions and forms of worship, and other human traditions, lives the one church. Its unity is also hidden under the divisions of Christianity. The one church is purely an article of faith, and yet it is a great reality in the world.

7

The last-quoted passage from the Apology clearly illumines the second part of our Article VII:

> For it is sufficient for the true unity of the Christian church that the Gospel be preached in conformity with a pure understanding of it and that the sacraments be administered in accordance with the divine Word. It is not necessary for the true unity of the Christian church that ceremonies, instituted by men, should be observed uniformly in all places. It is as Paul says in Eph. 4:4, 5, "There is one body and one Spirit, just as you were called to the one hope that belongs to your call, one Lord, one faith, one baptism [Tappert, p. 32; German text].

There is hardly a passage in our Confessions that has evoked more discussion than this one, and still today it is in the middle of the debates and controversies about the church and church unity, about confession and union, about the rights and wrongs of the modern ecumenical movement.

In our discussions of the first part of Article VII we rejected the division into visible and invisible church, as though the opening sentence speaks of the one holy church which continues forever (*una sancta ecclesia perpetuo mansura*), the invisible church, and the second sentence speaks of the congregation of the saints *congregatio sanctorum*, in which the means of grace are used, the visible church. There is only one church, of which one can speak in a strict sense or in a wider sense. Thus it is here. The true unity of the church, of which Article VII speaks, is both an article of faith and a reality in the world. It is the unity which binds together all those, wherever they may be in the world from the rising to the setting of the sun, who truly believe, who have one Christ, one Holy Spirit, one Gospel, one Baptism, and one Sacrament of the Altar, whether they have or do not have the same ceremonies or traditions. They have one Christ and one Holy Spirit because they have one Gospel, one Baptism, and one Sacrament of the Altar.

That is exactly the thought in Ephesians 4, whose interpretation is given in Article VII. Also there we find next to one another "one body and one Spirit . . . one hope . . . one Lord, one faith, one baptism, one God and Father" [vv. 4–6]. The one Gospel appears in the words, "just as you were called to the one hope that belongs to your call." (Compare Luther's explanation of the Third Article: "called . . . through the Gospel.") In and through the means of grace we have the one Lord, the one Spirit, the one God and Father. Since the means of grace create the church as the people of God, the body of Christ, the temple of the Holy Spirit, the *congregatio*, therefore they are also the marks of the church, the (*notae ecclesiae*).

Luther expands the list of the marks of the church. In *On the Councils and the Church* he lists the marks by which one can recognize "the Christian holy people": the Word of God, Baptism, the Sacrament of the Altar, the Office of the Keys. "Fifth, the church is recognized externally by the fact that it consecrates or calls ministers." "Sixth, the holy Christian people are externally recognized by prayer, public praise, and thanksgiving to God." "Seventh, the holy Christian people are externally recognized by the holy possession of the sacred cross. They must endure every misfortune and persecution, all kinds of trials and evil from the devil, the world, and the flesh . . . in order to become like their head, Christ. And the only reason they must suffer is that they steadfastly adhere to Christ and God's word, enduring this for the sake of Christ" (WA 50, 628, 632, 641 f. [American Edition 41, 148, 154, 164 f.]). These additional marks of the church belong with the first. Where the Word of God, the Gospel, is, there it demands to be preached; so there must be a ministry. Where the Gospel is, there people must come together for divine service in order to hear it. Where the Word is, there the cross must also be; otherwise how could the word of the cross be taken seriously? Where the Word and the sacraments are, there are God's holy people. "For the Word of God is living and active, sharper than any two-edged sword . . . discerning the thoughts and intentions of the heart" (Heb. 4:12). It is "like fire . . . and like a hammer which breaks the rock in pieces" (Jer. 23:29). It has God's promise that it will not return empty [Is. 55:10–11]. And Christ's sacraments are not just some things that men do. In them Christ Himself is present and active.

Because this is so, therefore the doctrine of Article VII immediately becomes an assignment, just as in Eph. 4 doctrine and exhortation, indicative and imperative, go together. Because there is one body and one Spirit, because you were called by the Gospel to one hope, because you have received the one Baptism of the one Lord in one faith, therefore "I . . . a prisoner for the Lord, beg you to lead a life worthy of the calling to which you have been called . . . eager to maintain the unity of the Spirit in the bond of peace" [vv. 1, 3]. So faith in the one church must immediately lead to eager preservation of that unity. The indicative and imperative go inseparably together also in Article VII. The great *satis est*, "it is sufficient for the true unity of the Christian church," involves a *necesse est*, it is necessary. As the life of the Christian is continually threatened by the temptation to sin and to fall away from the faith, and each day we are to return to our Baptism, daily repent, so the existence of the church is threatened by the devil, the world, and the flesh, in which we live also as members of the church. And the church must daily pray: "Lord Jesus Christ, will you not stay?" Daily, for the evening of the world draws on, let us plead with the hymn of our fathers which was so important to us in the church struggle in Germany:

Lord Jesus Christ, will you not stay?
It is now toward the end of day.
Oh, let your Word, that saving light,
Shine forth undimmed into the night.
(*Lutheran Worship*, 344)

Things would be better with the Lutheran Church around the world if we all, pastors and congregations, in all church bodies called Lutheran, would pray thus every evening.

8

So then the great article of the Augsburg Confession about the church is both a confession of firm faith in the indestructibility of the church and a call quickening our consciences to preserve the unity of the church and to restore it where it has been lost among us. The Apology calls the article of faith about the catholic [or universal] church "very comforting and highly necessary" [Par. 9, German text; *Concordia Triglotta*, p. 229]. How often has it not appeared as if the church were done for? *Ne desperemus*, "that we may not despair" (Par. 9 [Tappert, p. 170), we are given the great and comforting article of faith in the actuality of God's church in the world.

It would be an utter contradiction of all that the Augsburg Confession says in confessing what God's Word says, if we would use all this as a resting ground for our complacency. The confessors of Augsburg did not rest content with the fact that, despite all that was wrong in the papacy, the church was still there. They were not content to confess the profound inner communion of all God's children which no one can destroy. They were active in doing what they could to preserve the unity of outward Christianity. They took up the emperor's words regarding the purpose of their coming together to deal with the questions of the faith at the Diet, "to live together in unity and in one fellowship and church, even as we are all enlisted under one Christ" [AC Introduction, 4; Tappert, p. 25].

The question they then had to answer was wherein the true unity of the church consists. On the basis of God's Word they confessed that it is not to be found in unity of traditions or ceremonies but in the one Gospel and in the sacraments instituted by our Lord. They declined the false view of the church's unity which sees this unity in what human beings have arranged or devised, such as a great constitution or a uniform liturgy.

Our church has never taught that in areas such as these there *have* to be differences. On the contrary, there have always been efforts to preserve unity also in these areas. The confessors raised no basic objection against episcopal polity. They even acknowledged that the office of the pope was acceptable, if only pope and bishops would honor the

Gospel and not set themselves up as more than incumbents of the office of the Word and the sacraments. There was no objection to adding to this divine office also the humanly devised office of oversight (*episkopē*) over pastors and congregations. What the confessors could not do was heed the pope and the bishops more than the Word of God.

The Augsburg Confession makes this final declaration:

> St. Peter forbids the bishops to exercise lordship as if they had power to coerce the churches according to their will. It is not our intention to find ways of reducing the bishops' power, but we desire and pray that they may not coerce our consciences to sin. If they are unwilling to do this and ignore our petition, let them consider how they will answer for it in God's sight, inasmuch as by their obstinacy they offer occasion for division and schism, which they should in truth help to prevent (AC XXVIII, 76 ff. [Tappert, p. 94]).

Thus the Lutheran Reformation ended with the division of Christendom; the efforts to preserve unity ended in the separation of those on both sides who were "all enlisted under one Christ" and so wished to live "in one fellowship and church," as was confessed in the introduction of the Augsburg Confession.

Why was no other outcome possible? We can answer this question only by referring to the deep mystery of world and church history that, in this sinful world, where lies are fathered on every hand, what is lie and what is truth cannot be known if there is no line between them. Therefore unity in the church is possible only with demarcation against heresy. Thus when our Lord prayed for the unity of all those who believe in Him, He also prayed: "Sanctify them in the truth; Thy Word is truth" [John 17:17]. The apostle John was then a servant of the truth, and so a servant of the true unity of the church, when he drew the line against those who denied the Incarnation. This was also the case when the early church drew the line against Marcion and the Gnostics, Athanasius drew it against the Arians, Augustine against Pelagius, and Luther against the pope, Zwingli, and the Anabaptists. So it has ever been with the church militant in this world. We cannot confess what is true without rejecting what contradicts it. Kierkegaard observed that truth's quotation marks are polemical.

And when here on earth the tragic case occurs, which happens again and again where the question of truth is earnestly engaged, that one confession of faith is set against another, conscience against conscience, then we must leave the decision to Him who in the Last Judgment will finally separate truth from error. We do not know God's judgments, and can and may not anticipate them. Also when we must speak the *damnamus* ("we condemn") against a false teaching, God's forgiving grace may bring the erring sinner into the church triumphant, where there is no more untruth. On the other hand, this door will be shut to many a one who has done battle for the truth in perfect orthodoxy, but has forgotten that he too was only a poor sinner who lives only by forgiving grace. Only in God's light, when we shall no longer "know in part" but "shall understand fully, even as" we "have been fully understood" [1 Cor. 13:12]—only then, and not before, will we in the full truth of God also fully understand the true unity of the church.

9

If this, in bold strokes, is the Lutheran doctrine of the church and its unity, *what does this doctrine mean for Lutheranism today?* What tasks does it impose upon us? The first great task is obviously a profound self-examination. Such an examination was evident in what we cited above from the assembly of the Evangelical Lutheran Conference of 1868. "The wounds we have inflicted upon ourselves in ignorance or unfaithfulness" are still bleeding, and they have been multiplied in the decades that have passed since then. In territory after territory Lutheranism in Germany has been displaced, until today it lives unambiguously only in the free churches. Who is responsible for this?

The Lutherans in the Lutheran territorial churches have gone the way of the Lutherans in the Union churches who banded together (*Vereinslutheraner*) and committed themselves to confess the Lutheran faith. They declared that when this or that demand would be made upon them, that then the occasion for confession (*casus confessionis*) would have arrived and they would not yield. But then they did yield, saying that this was not the right *casus confessionis*. That is how it went every time. They gave up one position after another. They claimed they were indeed always ready to confess; yet when it came to it, they accepted everything. It was a tragic history, this history of the efforts to recover the Lutheran Church in Prussia. Many hearts were broken, and not only because of sorrow over a course of events they could not stop, but also because of shame at their own failure.

They then set their hope on the territorial churches that were still Lutheran: Saxony, Hannover, Bavaria, Württemberg. But even there what was Lutheran was in rapid decline. One generation ago there was still a scattering of confessional Lutherans in Württemberg. Where are they today? And what of Hannover and Bavaria? The German Evangelical Church Federation turned out to be what was prophesied by a shrewd leader of the Union churches. He called it "the sleeping car in which the Lutherans are traveling into the Union." It did not have to be that way, but the man knew the condition of Lutheran confession in the nominally still Lutheran churches.

There came the year 1933, and with it the German Evangelical Church, under Nazi compulsion. But who can compel a bishop to deny his faith? In the following year the Lutheran bishops in Barmen ratified this church, which for Barth and all the Reformed, for Niemöller and all the Union people, was a genuine union. Barth called it a confessional union (*Bekenntnisunion*).

Then came the day when Hitler's thousand-year *Reich* came to an end. It was the last occasion when the Lutheran bishops in Germany might have confessed with their deeds. They missed also this opportunity, and their churches were swallowed up in the new union called the Evangelical Church in Germany (*Evangelische Kirche in Deutschland* [EKiD]). In Eisenach, at the foot of the Wartburg, the Lutheran Church in Germany was buried in 1948. Löhe's nightmare of the Lutheran Church being buried by its own pastors became a reality. From the sleeping car of the Church Federation it was still possible to get out. One can leave a Church Federation. From the grave of the EKiD no one rises again. This hybrid between federation and church, a federation which calls itself a church and acts as a church, a church which would be a federation—"federationist church" (*bündische Kirche*) they said in 1933—recognizes no right of secession. The VELKD [Vereinigte Evangelisch-Lutherische Kirche Deutschlands, United Evangelical Lutheran Church of Germany], which was formed within the Evangelical Church in Germany, cannot get out of the larger structure, even if it wanted to. It does not want to, because it knows it cannot.

Meanwhile the Lutheran churches of the world have been looking on as spectators. They do not realize that by their being content to be deedless spectators they seal their own fate. In Sweden the slumbering conscience of a minority awakened when the demand that women be ordained was voted approval by a majority of the bishops and the church assembly. But what was there to do? The state used pressure to bring it about, and so on every hand we hear lamentation over the tyranny of the state. The state, however, can point out that the church made no use of the possibility of rejecting laws decided by the state. Opposition has been shown by the Assembly for the Church (*Kyrklige Samling*) and the bishop of Gothenburg, Bo Giertz. They are carrying on the struggle in exactly the same way as did the Lutherans in Germany and in the Prussian Union, hoping that, after winter, spring must come. The rule for the seasons is not, however, the rule in church history. A confessional church does not happen if one does not actually confess. It is not enough to work out a casuistry of how pastors and laity are to react when one of the new priestesses appears in church. Nothing less will do than taking the stand that all such ordinations are contrary to God's Word and invalid, and that all official acts done by these ladies are done by lay persons. Baptisms done by them stand as those done by a midwife. Those who walk the corridors of power will not be slow to react to such a stand. When they apply their disciplinary measures, there may then be such joy as Görres expressed in his *Athanasius* upon the imprisonment of the archbishop of Cologne: "Praise be to Jesus Christ; now there is violence!" Thus churches are saved.

Such hope dies when men are silent as our Confession is dismantled piece by piece, as the place for being a Lutheran in the traditional structure of the Lutheran Church is constricted more and more, as God's Word is set aside. Such silence means the end of the Lutheran Church. No one would claim it to be a fact that the churches of Germany, Sweden, Denmark, Norway, and Finland are inwardly held together by "great unanimity" [AC I, 1] in "the teaching of the Gospel and the administration of the sacraments" [AC VII, 2]. There is no longer a consensus in these churches regarding what God's Word demands, what the Gospel actually is, what Baptism and the Lord's Supper are. What holds them together is the setup they have inherited, their constitutions and their apparatus for running things, their property and the money that the state provides or collects for them. These are the "human traditions or rites and ceremonies" [AC VII, 3]. They are not what Article VII of the Augsburg Confession says creates the true unity of the church.

In the Prussian Union and then in the other churches it was at first said that what everything really depends on is the preaching of the Gospel and the administration of the sacraments. It was said that no pastor was being prevented from preaching the Gospel in truth and purity and from rightly administering the sacraments [AC VII, 2]. On the contrary, that was said to be what was desired.

Whatever one may think of the details in Kliefoth's address in 1868, he was surely right in rejecting the view that what is said in Article VII of the Augsburg Confession applies only to pastors, with those who govern the church excepted. For what else does it mean to govern the affairs of the church than to exercise the pastoral office in areas that extend beyond the local congregation? A bishop is one who preaches and administers the sacraments. He ordains in the name of the church. He puts the vows to the ordinands that they will be faithful to Scripture and the Lutheran Confessions. What sort of hypocrisy is it when I obligate a man to a confession which I myself do not believe! That is what used to go on in Prussia, although today it is generally regarded as intolerable. It was the way of the Prussian Union also in the Rhineland, in areas where there were both Lutherans and Reformed. Those who were training to be teachers of religion had to learn both Luther's Catechism and the Heidelberg Catechism so that they could teach the one or the other as needed. And what of those training to be pastors, when they are taught by men who do not confess their church's confession? What of their preaching of the Gospel and administration of the sacraments, and their ordination vow?

Let no one say that confession is not mentioned in Article VII as a mark of the church. No, not expressly. But what is a confession if it is no longer the declaration of the church: This is what we believe, teach, and confess, because it is the true doctrine of the Gospel, because it is Biblical truth to be preached from every pulpit!

If our fathers of 1868 could speak to us today, what a preaching of repentance that would be for the whole Lutheran Church, or what is left of it.

10

This call to repentance would go out not only to the Lutherans of Germany and Europe, but certainly to them first. They allowed the Lutheran Church to disappear as church in one territory after another until little more is left than a viewpoint or a school of thought in theology—until this also dies. For schools of thought in theology soon pass away; they disappear with their teachers and leaders. Is it conceivable that ever again in Sweden, and perhaps also in Denmark and Norway, a man might become a professor or a bishop if he saw the ordination of women as defection from the Word of God? Is there any German university today where men would be tolerated who reject the Unions, including those of Barmen in 1933 and 1934, and the Evangelical Church in Germany (EKiD) in 1948, declaring them not only false in theory but actually breaking off fellowship with such Union churches? Such questions can be put in ways appropriate to each of the European state and territorial churches, also where they are no longer governed directly by the state, but where the church authorities are at the pleasure of the mass of indifferent and nominal church members. It is the tragic but irreversible outcome of European church history: A state church can no longer be a confessional church. But a church can be Lutheran only as it is a confessional church.

This is a fact for our brothers in the faith in *America* to ponder. Are they even aware of it? Do they recognize the great crisis of the church of the Lutheran Confession? If one looks closely at the Lutheran churches in America and studies their development, one finds little awareness of the crisis. Where was their witness in 1933 and 1934 to warn and to encourage us? What was their witness in 1948? Many sat by quietly; they thought it unloving to get mixed up in the affairs of other churches. The representatives of the Missouri Synod felt they should not repeat the mistakes of earlier times and give criticism that was not always well informed or loving. But it is never a service of love if one does not help a sick man out of his sickness, but says to him that all is well. We are all responsible for one another, we who have before God and the whole church confessed the Unaltered Augsburg Confession or the Book of Concord. We are not unknown to each other. Most of the Lutheran churches in America are members together with the European Lutheran churches in the Lutheran World Federation. They see, or they ought to see, what is going on there. They cannot but see how the Confessions have become little more than a formality for many. They cannot be ignorant of what is taught in the member churches. Have things gone so far that our American brothers in the faith recognize the ordination of women? Or is this to be regarded as an internal matter for each church by itself? What has been heard from the Lutheran churches of America as they have watched one church after another welcomed into membership in the Federation, some of whom do not call themselves Lutheran, some who quickly put on the name? Subscription to the constitution of the Federation may be lightly done; many churches have no intention of considering the doctrine of the Augsburg Confession as that doctrine, and no other, which is to be preached and taught, have no commitment to guard this doctrine or repudiate what contradicts it.

Such a commitment might honestly be expected. No one can expect that all pastors become paragons of Lutheran confession and preaching by tomorrow. In every church there is weakness and theological ignorance. Yet of those churches which declare that they are Lutheran one can expect that they will learn, live, and grow from the resources of the Lutheran Confessions, and so will become what they confess themselves to be. The sickness at the heart of the Lutheran World Federation is the untruthfulness which appears symptomatically in so many of its decisions. For too many modern church leaders, church politics comes first, and then the Confessions become a tool of church politics.

This is what the Lutherans of America should have seen. Why did they not notice it? A hundred years ago they saw such things quite clearly. The '60s of the last century saw a great decision in American Lutheranism. It is connected with the name of Samuel Simon Schmucker (1799—1873). He was the first president of the first Lutheran seminary in America (Gettysburg, founded in 1826), and he held that office for four decades. He was prominent in the General Synod, a product of the pietistic and unionistic Lutheranism in Pennsylvania influenced by August Hermann Francke. In general American church history he is known as one of the prophets of the Ecumenical Movement in the United States. He is the father of what was called "federative union," a combination of churches that retain their identity and yet enter into church fellowship. For such a combination with the Reformed, the Methodists, and other Protestants, he wrote a confession of 12 articles. It was composed of pieces taken from the Anglican articles, the Methodist Discipline, Lutheran and Reformed confessions, and from the articles of the Brethren. His influence in the efforts to achieve church unions in America seems to have been greater than was formerly supposed. He is one of those who prepared the way for today's National Council of the Churches of Christ in the U.S.A.

In Lutheranism he is not highly regarded. In 1854 he published his *Definite Platform*, a watered-down Augsburg Confession from which the specifically Lutheran doctrines had been removed. His goal was an "American Lutheranism," indigenous and living in harmonious fellowship with the Reformed Churches. At this all the Lutheran synods, also his own, turned away from him. Whatever differences there were among them, here they stood united: They would not let themselves be robbed of the Unaltered Augsburg Confession. That was the great decision which happened in the '60s only a hundred years ago.

Could something like that happen now? The situation is again fraught with heavy debate of weighty church issues. Is it possible to repeat what was done a hundred years ago? And if it did happen again, would it be more than an action of church politics in which for practical reasons an old confession would once more be formally affirmed without thereby making a decision of faith? To accept a confession, when this is seriously done, means to make a decision about what is believed, for the individual and for the church body.

Do we still understand our ordination that way? When a congregation or church in America espouses the Augsburg Confession, is this still understood in the sense of a decision as to what is believed? Or have things gone so far also among the Lutherans of America that the church's confession is only something that has to be said if you are writing up a constitution? To be sure, the Confessions should be preserved, and why not? Who would want to throw out such a precious old piece of furniture? If the Anglicans pledge all their ministers to the Thirty-Nine Articles, the Presbyterians to the Westminster Confession, and Roman Catholics to the Profession of Faith of the Council of Trent, why should we Lutherans not do the same with the Unaltered Augsburg Confession? There was once in Oxford a wise and much-honored Anglican churchman. When he was asked how he could accept the Thirty-Nine Articles along with his Catholic convictions, he replied, "I also accept the gas company of Oxford, but I do not approve of it."

Have we Lutherans also reached this level of wisdom, resignation, or despair? In any case, this is something we ought to be quite clear about: Our church was the last of the Reformation churches still loyal to its Confessions. For innumerable Christians the Augsburg Confession has been truly their confession. If it should now sink to the level of being only a historical document, a formality to be put in a constitution, then we ought to know that the Profession of Faith of the Council of Trent and the doctrine of the Vatican Council will continue to stand as the confession of innumerable millions of human beings. There the faith confessed at the Reformation is included—but among the false doctrines that are put under the anathema!

That the foregoing picture is not overdrawn is clear from the facts which are there for anyone to see. In America the Lutherans are now mostly in three large groups. The Lutheran Church in America is putting itself together out of the United Lutheran Church, the Augustana Church (Swedish origins), plus one formerly Danish and another Finnish church. That adds up to one third of the Lutherans. This church characterizes itself by its participation not only in the Lutheran World Federation but also in the World Council of Churches and in the National Council of the Churches of Christ in the U.S.A., in which American Protestantism finds its unity. The churches in the middle are now united in The American Lutheran Church (The ALC). This church also belongs to the World Council of Churches, but not yet to the National Council of the Churches of Christ in the U.S.A. With the first-named church it forms the National Lutheran Council.

In all these churches there are still faithful Lutherans. To what extent they form a viewpoint that has become a minority is not clear. Those from the former Evangelical Lutheran Church who took their confession seriously were not able to halt the entry of the new American Lutheran Church into the World Council of Churches. What the "left" [LCA] and the "center" [The ALC] have in common in spite of all existing differences is that they recognize all the European state and territorial churches, even the most liberal, and beyond what is Lutheran extend their recognition to churches that in fact operate as Union churches. They work together with all of them in the Lutheran World Federation. Beyond that, they acknowledge the World Council of Churches and work with it, holding prominent positions. To what extent the confessional consciousness of these churches has been shattered is shown by every issue of their church papers, every decision these churches make. The number of pastors whose pledge to the Book of Concord is without reservation (*quia*) becomes less from year to year; or if they do it, they do not know what that means. Among the young pastors in all these churches there is a growing discussion of the question whether the old Confessions can still be accepted as their fathers accepted them a generation or two ago. It is openly stated that this is no longer possible.

What is happening here is tied up with the loss of the doctrine of Holy Scripture as the Word of God inspired by the Holy Spirit. Those on the left no longer dare say that Scripture is the Word of God, as is evidenced by the explanation accompanying the union documents. The old doctrine is still there in the constitution of The American Lutheran Church; those who did not want it there kept quiet so as not to hinder the union. Pietism once made its way through Europe traveling from west to east, from one church to another, undermining the doctrinal substance of the confessional churches, and so preparing the way for the Rationalism that brought the dissolution of the Christian faith. Similarly we may observe the deadly disease of a new, doctrinally indifferent Enthusiasm running its course in America. It draws strength from religious and intellectual thought in the United States and from the ever-more-powerful Ecumenical Movement. We know enough about such spiritual epidemics from the history of our own time! The sickness which has ravaged Lutheranism in the Eastern states now takes its course in the Midwest, traditionally a fortress of confessional Lutheranism. Iowa and Ohio have already fallen victim to it; the symptoms are evident in their faculties.

Now the sickness rages in Missouri, and unless there are signs and wonders this last great church of confessional Lutheranism will succumb. The churches of the left and the middle are simply waiting for Missouri. They see that the Synodical Conference with its continual internal tensions cannot last much longer, and their hope is that Missouri will then move into the National Lutheran Council, and from there into the Lutheran World Federation and the World Council of Churches. No one can tell what would then happen with the remaining Lutheranism (Wisconsin, the Norwegians, and the Slovaks of the Synodical Conference), or what might split off from Missouri and from other churches. Everything is waiting for the fall of Missouri. Then the way would finally be open for a Lutheran world church without a confession.

11

Without a confession? Yes, without a confession. For what most Lutherans in America understand by a confession is not what the confessing Lutheran Church has always understood by that term. Rather it is what Schmucker meant by it, what Dr. Fry and perhaps most of the leaders of world Lutheranism mean by it: sentences in which Christians or churches express the convictions they share. It is indeed important to know how much we share. This is especially true in this time of chaos in churches and theologies. We must know what we share with others, and what we do not share. We must pursue serious doctrinal discussion with those from whom we are separated, in order that on the basis of Holy Scripture we may be brought to one common doctrine.

Such theses, however, are still no confession. To suppose that they are is a notion which can be traced back to a fatal misunderstanding of Article VII that one encounters again and again. It goes something like this: For church unity it is enough "to agree concerning the teaching of the Gospel and the administration of the sacraments" (*consentire de doctrina evangelii et de administratione sacramentorum*). If we find that we agree with others regarding our understanding of the Gospel and the administration of the sacraments, then we can establish church fellowship with them. This may happen church with church, or even congregation with congregation and individual with individual. This last comes under the heading of "selective fellowship," as it is called in America. Two pastors or congregations of different churches who live together in one place find that they believe the same, and on the basis of this consensus they enter upon church fellowship with each other. Since tomorrow one or both of the pastors may be called elsewhere and the makeup of the congregations is changing, this means the atomizing of the church. This is especially the case when both sides are weak in faith and theology. What is regarded as a consensus in doctrine may in fact be a consensus of ignorance and poverty of doctrine. There are even those who suppose that they can establish degrees of unity. The degrees match the level of agreement reached so far in the discussions. The consensus one tries to read out of Article VII is in all such cases a purely human arrangement.

It is a remarkable fact that until quite recently there was no translation of the German text of the Augsburg Confession, or at least not one that was widely known. The English text of the *Concordia Triglotta*, the three-language edition of the Book of Concord, takes into account both the German and the Latin versions in the case of all the other confessions, but not so with the Augsburg Confession. Here only the Latin goes into the English text. In the English translation of the Book of Concord which was recently published in Philadelphia [the Tappert Edition], a translation is given of both the Latin and the German versions of the Augsburg Confession. The German version, however, has not been quite fully understood. The great "It is enough" (*satis est*) is clearly directed against Rome. For the unity of the church Rome required more than unity in the faith; it required the acceptance of human traditions and ceremonies. *Satis est* does not then postulate a minimum of agreement, a consensus, which we achieve in the course of our discussions, but a maximum: " . . . that [with one accord, *einträchtiglich*] the Gospel be preached *in conformity with a pure understanding of it* and that the sacraments be administered in accordance with the divine Word" [italics Dr. Sasse's]. Not the agreement in doctrine—the Roman church has a consensus in doctrine, the Baptists also have one; every church has some sort of consensus, even if it is a consensus in agreeing that doctrine is not important—but only the consensus in the *pure* doctrine and in the *right* administration of the sacraments is the consensus demanded in the Augsburg Confession. That is the "great unanimity" (*magnus consensus*) with which the first article of the Augsburg Confession begins, a consensus not made by men but given by God, the consensus in the right faith, which only the Holy Spirit creates.

If it were only a human consensus, then the doctrinal decisions of the Confession would have validity only for Lutheran Churches. Then it would only claim to be the doctrine of a particular church, just as other churches have their own particular confessions. There is nothing of this said anywhere in the Book of Concord. It has no notion of any such thing as a Lutheran Church. We do not believe in the Lutheran Church, but in the one, holy, catholic [or universal] church. The Book of Concord actually became the confession of a particular church. It was first called Evangelical, then Evangelical Lutheran, and also Lutheran. But that only came as a consequence of the way things developed in the Reformation's history. It was a consequence of the church division which could not be stopped.

We believe that the true church is wherever the Gospel is still heard and where Christ's sacraments are present. Thus the archconfessionalist Philipp Nicolai believed that Christ's church was present among the Muscovites, the Ethiopians, and in the churches of the Jesuits in America [Werner Elert, *The Structure of Lutheranism*, pp. 391 ff., Note 8]. But to establish church fellowship with those who mix this Gospel with false doctrine, that we cannot do, not even with Lutherans who deny the faith of their fathers, as little as Philipp Nicolai could have church fellowship with the Muscovites and the Jesuits.

This does not mean that our Confession can claim to have some sort of infallibility. It does not mean that all Christians must first accept the Book of Concord before we can have church fellowship with them. We are bound together with the true church of all ages in the great consensus of what is believed, taught, and confessed, also with those who did not yet have or need an Augsburg Confession. We are also bound up in the unity of the true church with those who after us will confess the true faith even to the end of the world, whether they use the words of our Confession or say it in other ways. But it must be the same faith, for there is only one Gospel. This faith embraces the great Biblical truths which were set down in our Confession in defense against false doctrine and in obedience to the Lord who looks to us all to confess His everlasting truth, until He confesses before His heavenly Father those who have confessed Him and His Gospel in this world.

Evening is falling also upon the Lutheran Church. But in the evening the Lord of His church is perhaps most near.

68

MINISTRY AND CONGREGATION

Letters to Lutheran Pastors, No. 8
July 1949

1

One of the most grievous events in the history of the Lutheran Church in the 19th century was the fact that the two great churchmen Wilhelm Löhe and Ferdinand Walther went separate ways after the great theological leader of the Missouri Synod had in 1851 had a most promising meeting with Löhe in Neuendettelsau.

That the theological faculty at Erlangen had small regard for both of them means little. However great the achievements of the old Erlangen School, however great its representatives as men and as scholars, there was yet a weakness there which rendered them incapable of being a resource for a lasting renewal of the Lutheran Church. They were unable to hold themselves clear of the insidious poison of Schleiermacherian subjectivism. Although they were dedicated to discern and defend the objective truths of revelation, Schleiermacher's way of doing theology had infected and weakened them. What at the time was already recognized by some clear-sighted men became only too obvious by the end of the century. If "I the Christian am to me the theologian the most proper matter of my study" [J. C. K. von Hofmann of the Erlangen School, *Schriftbeweis*, I, 10], then no power on earth could keep theology from becoming a study of things in man, a "science of religion."

The other great weakness of the Erlangen School was their being so bound up in the little world of Germany's territorial churches. Their horizon reached from their small town in Franconia toward the south as far as Nürnberg and Munich, and northwards to Leipzig, Dresden, Rostock, and even as far as Dorpat [Tartu in Estonia]. How vastly farther-reaching was the vision and engagement of the little village pastor in Neuendettelsau. How much more clearly Löhe and Walther saw what faced the Lutheran Church in the world—beyond a Lutheran Church run by a bureaucracy that was watched over and guided by the state. For them the church was not just a department of the state. No one could imagine that out of the laborious work of organizing these congregations on the fringes of civilization would come the great churches in whose hands, so far as it lies in human hands, today rests the future of Lutheranism. So also no one could foresee the consequences of the break between Walther and Löhe, between Missouri and Iowa. We see these consequences today and are faced with the question whether the agreement which failed to happen at that time might come in our day.

2

What separated Löhe and Walther, and so what separated Missouri and Iowa, was not by any means only the relationship between church and ministry, but this was certainly a primary point in which they could not find agreement. Nor was it a matter which separated only these two men and the churches they represented. The separation ran right through Lutheranism. In the second third of the 19th century Lutherans were drawn, in their own way, into the deep-going discussion which at that time involved all of Christendom, from the Roman Catholics before the Vatican I to the strangest sects of the Reformed world (for instance the Irvingites and the Disciples of Christ), and profoundly affected Anglicanism.

One can at first only marvel that Lutheranism could have been so disturbed by this question, even to the point of causing divisions in the Prussian Free Church and her daughter church in Australia. For the Lutheran Church, matters of church government belong to the adiaphora, to the "rites and ceremonies, instituted by men" (Augsburg Confession VII), concerning which there may and must be freedom in the church. Christ is not the legislator of a human religious fellowship, and the Gospel has in it no law which prescribes the only right way of organization and polity for the church.

One must be clear as to what this means. Other churches have "an order by which the Lord wills the church to be governed," as Calvin put it [*Institutes*, 4, 3, 1; LCC 41, 1053]. This is true of all Catholic churches, both of the East and of the West, and of all Reformed churches. Their differences have to do only with what that order must be—the universal monarchy of the pope, the episcopal-synodical government of the church as in the Eastern churches and Anglicanism, a ruling senate of presbyters among whom there must be no differences of rank, or the autonomy of the individual congregation as in Congregationalism and among the Baptists. These are just a few notable options, all of which claim to represent what the New Testament requires for the polity of the church.

Luther's entire greatness and the boldness of his basic theological principle of the strict separation of Law and Gospel become evident when one sees how beyond all these possibilities he goes his lonesome way: Christ gave His church no such law prescribing one right organization, government, and polity (*de constituenda ecclesia*). Any way of organizing things may do, so long as the means of grace are going on and are not frustrated.

One thing the Lord gave His church, however, belongs not only to its well-being *bene esse* but to its very being *esse:* "In order that we may obtain this faith, the ministry of teaching the Gospel and administering the sacraments was instituted," says Article V of the Augsburg Confession. In order that we may obtain the justifying faith of which the previous article has spoken, the Gospel must be preached, the sacraments must be administered. Therefore God has instituted the ministry, the service through which this happens. Wherever the means of grace are rightly administered, there God fulfills His promise that the Word will not return empty, there faith is created, there is the church, the congregation of saints, of justified sinners.

How the congregation organizes itself, for this no prescriptions are given, just as there are none for how the church's ministry is to be organized. The apostles came to recognize that it would be helpful for their ministry if they were relieved of the work of caring for the poor and attending to money matters. So the office of the deacons was created as an auxiliary office. But the church was the church already before this office was created. So the church can at any time create auxiliary offices to meet the needs of the time. Examples of this in the history of the church are the office of an episcopate, or superintendency, or any other offices, whatever they may be called. But all these offices have their right of existence only insofar as they serve the one great office of the preaching of the Gospel and the administering of the sacraments. A bishop may be entrusted with the task of seeing to the running of a great diocese. But the meaning of such an assignment can only consist in this, that he thereby gives room and support to the church's ministry. His actual office is the office of pastor, also when he is a pastor for

71

pastors. By human arrangement he may have the work of superintendency. By divine mandate he has solely the office of preaching the forgiveness and justification of sinners for Christ's sake.

<h1 style="text-align:center">3</h1>

If this is something on which there is agreement in the whole Lutheran Church, if the Lutheran Church can live with a consistorial or
an episcopal constitution, if, as in America, it can live with a presby-
terial-synodical or sometimes even an almost completely congregational
organization, how are we to explain the differences of opinion which
exactly in the question of ministry and congregation, and thereby in the
question of church organization, have repeatedly split our church since
Löhe and Walther went their separate ways?

This is a hard question to answer. It seems to me there is no doubt
that Lutheranism was infiltrated by the organization and polity problems
of other churches and confessions. No church in the 19th century was
able to stay clear of such problems. We have only to name Möhler,
Newman, Pusey, Vinet, and Chalmers. All confessions of Christendom
were affected. It was a time when the old Christian Europe seemed to
be coming to an end, and the question was what would take its place.

We Lutherans have much to learn from the passionate struggle of
Roman Catholicism to be free from the fetters of the state shaped by
the Enlightenment. This church's struggle, for instance in Cologne, has
instructive parallels with the confessional battle of the Prussian Lutherans, just as later the brave struggle of the Hessian *Renitenz* [a
confessional Lutheran movement] has parallels to the *Kulturkampf* at
the time of Bismarck. We do well to study the tragic story of the Trac-
tarian Movement in England, the gripping history of the Disruption in
Scotland, and parallel movements on the other side of the Atlantic
Ocean.

With all of this going on, Lutheranism did not remain wholly true
to the glorious freedom of the Reformation. If everywhere the question
was being urged as to what is the authentic way of organizing the church,
the way prescribed by Christ, the way required by the Bible, then our
church was caught in the danger of wanting to give an answer to this
question. With all their faithfulness to the Lutheran Confessions, neither
Walther nor Löhe (to name just these two) succeeded in escaping this
danger.

It is similar to what happened with our classical dogmaticians in
the Age of Orthodoxy. They were drawn into answering questions which

came from Calvinism or Roman Catholicism, without recognizing that these were falsely put. Take for example the question of the visible and invisible church, which still continues to plague us. The fathers in the Age of Orthodoxy, as well as the fathers in the 19th century, were drawn into Reformed terminology on this question. They failed to recognize that Luther's *ecclesia abscondita* [cf. "The Church is hidden" (WA 18, 652; American Edition 33, 89)] is not quite the same as the *ecclesia invisibilis* ["invisible church"] of the Reformed. The Lutheran dogmaticians would therefore have done better to have kept to the expressions used in the Confessions and by Luther. To be sure, when we confess the church we are not confessing what we see (*Sehartikel*) but what we believe (*Glaubensartikel*). Our eyes cannot now see the church as the kingdom of Christ. As the Apology confesses (along with Luther) in expounding Articles VII and VIII of the Augsburg Confession, it is "hidden under the cross" (*sub cruce tectum* [18]). No human eye sees the church as the body of Christ. It is an eschatological fact which must be differentiated from the "association of outward ties and rites" (*societas externarum rerum ac rituum* [Apology VII and VIII, 5]) which we see. Insofar as this is so, the church may be spoken of as invisible. The expression "invisible church," however, comes from Augustine freighted with his ecclesiology, and further freight has been loaded onto it by Reformed theology. There are things here which we do not and cannot confess.

Why did they not stay with Luther's simple teaching of the "hidden" church? Here, as in some other points, our orthodox dogmaticians allowed themselves to become far too dependent on their opponents, and the theologians of the 19th century simply took this over. After all, they had no better Lutheran books of dogmatics than those from the Age of Orthodoxy. Where could they have found any such?

There is also something else to be considered. It is certainly true, as the Smalcald Articles confess, that "a seven-year-old child knows what the church is, namely, holy believers and sheep who hear the voice of their shepherd" (III, XII, 2). And yet the theologians of the last century were correct in expecting (as A. Vilmar repeatedly expressed it) that they might be led more deeply into the doctrine of the church as they were called upon to face the colossal catastrophes in the political and social life of their day and the impending future. From the beginning the church knew all that is confessed in the Nicene Creed, but it was by way of the gigantic struggle against ancient heathenism that the church of antiquity came to confess with such clarity that Jesus Christ is truly God and truly man. It is only in this way, and in no other, that we may speak of advance in the understanding of the faith.

Why the two great Lutheran streams in the last century did not flow together was clearly seen by Vilmar: The Lutheran Church had not yet come to full clarity as to what the articles in the Augsburg Confession about the church mean for the *life* of the church. So it came about that the great Lutherans of the last century left us a heritage not yet exhausted or made our own. This is especially true of those who did not just sit at their desks and think theoretically about the nature of the church, but were actively engaged in gathering and caring for congregations. The task which is given our generation cannot be to repeat the formulations of both sides and to take up the discussion where it came to a stop a century ago. Rather our task is again to think through what at that time remained unresolved. For this task we have the help of what the church has experienced since then and of what may have been given of deeper insight into the teachings of Holy Scripture.

4

It is truly remarkable how modern historical research into the beginnings of the way the church was organized has confirmed Luther's exegetical insight that the New Testament tells of no specific single way of organizing the church, and so no such single way can be canonized. As in the history of the liturgy so also in the history of the church's organization, the beginning was marked not by uniformity but by diversity. Therefore it was also possible to read into the New Testament the most diverse ways of organizing the church, and then to derive satisfaction in discovering them there!

Thus the doctrine of papal primacy was read into the Peter passages, although it had grown out of quite unbiblical soil. What Acts 15 tells us of the meeting of the council in Jerusalem has been burdened with the theory of the infallible synod, whose roots are not to be found in Scripture but in ancient sociology. The Catholic doctrine that while one may err but that all together cannot err is a notion that runs through the ancient world, from the Stoics right on to Mohammed. What do Calvin's presbyters have in common with the presbyters of the New Testament? What does "the church of God which is at Corinth" have in common with what Congregationalists nowadays understand by "congregation"? Paul would simply not be able to understand what the doctrine of the body of Christ as expressed in Pius XII's encyclical *Mystici*

Corporis has to do with what he teaches of the church as the body of Christ.

It is not surprising, then, that there is some uncertainty throughout Christendom as to the Scripturalness of the various church polities. Among the Reformed we no longer find the same certainty with which Calvin was able to find in the Bible "the order by which the Lord wills the church to be governed." We hear rather of a few basic lines laid down there that are viewed as obligatory (a presbytery as church senate or council of brothers, a synod as the final court of appeal, rejection of the office of bishop—even when, as in Hungary, this title is used because of state-church considerations). Even in Catholic dogmatics we find the attempt being made to soften the stark statements of Trent and Vatican I in order to bring them more into harmony with the historical facts recorded in the New Testament.

In this respect M. Schmaus's *Katholische Dogmatik* (1964) is most instructive. He observes "that Paul can describe the celebration of the Eucharist without any express mention of a particular priesthood (1 Cor. 11:17-34)," and then continues, "It is an action of the whole congregation in Corinth" (IV, 1, 728). After reading what the same dogmatician says so splendidly about the priestly character of the church (the priesthood of all believers), what he says about the special priesthood obtrudes like a foreign body in the whole context of his presentation. In support of the priesthood of all Christians numerous Bible passages are given; in support of the particular priesthood not a single one. There could not be a more convincing presentation of the unbiblical character of the Roman Catholic doctrine of the priesthood.

At another place we read of the relationship between presbyters and bishops: "The New Testament terms *presbyteroi* and *episcopoi* do not yet express different levels of order as do our words 'priest' and 'bishop,' which derive from these Greek designations. The separation of the one office, referred to with two names, meets us first in Ignatius of Antioch. Here for the first time we have clearly the division into three orders (deacons, priests, bishops). This may be traced back to about the year 100. Its seeds lie in the apostolic period" (p. 729). So only its seeds! To say it bluntly, the Catholic hierarchy is not yet there in the New Testament. At most it is a development of New Testamental seeds. Here we see how cautious a Catholic theologian, strictly bound to Roman dogma, has become when he deals with the Biblical foundations of the Roman doctrine regarding how the church must be constituted (*Kirchenverfassung*).

75

Today no one who takes seriously the Scriptural evidence would be so rash as to assert that there is to be found in the New Testament a set way of organizing the church which is obligatory for all time. This fact would surely be acknowledged by the Lutherans of the 19th century, although in their day they were not able altogether to resist the temptation to find an answer to the question as to how the church must be organized, even though they hedged their answers with all kinds of reservations and provisos. Today they would simply bow before the fact that in the church of the New Testament there were several possible ways of ordering the holy ministry and the church, the congregation of saints.

5

Which has the primacy, ministry or congregation? Is the office the product of the congregation, or is the congregation the product of the office? Löhe stood for the office, and in a different way also Vilmar and Kliefoth. Walther stood for the congregation. (Von Höfling does not fit in here; neither side took him seriously, and despite all his other accomplishments, he did not make a serious contribution in this matter.) There is more to this than is suggested by likening it to the question whether the hen comes from the egg or the egg from the hen. What is involved here is in fact of enormous theological importance. The entire understanding of the church depends on it.

When Walther and Missouri contended for the priority of the congregation, they could justly call on Luther and the old Lutheran Church as witnesses. In his *To the Christian Nobility* Luther gives the following well-known illustration of the doctrine of the priesthood of all believers. Some Christians find themselves in the desert. There is no ordained priest among them. They elect one of their number to the holy ministry. By this election he has whatever rights and responsibilities belong to one who occupies the church's ministry (WA 6, 407 [American Edition 44, 128]).

We may compare the certainty with which Luther speaks here with the uncertainty and indecision with which Thomas More dealt with the same problem a few years earlier in his *Utopia*. After an account of the tolerant Enlightenment religion of the Utopians and its kinship with Christianity as the enlightened humanist understood it, he relates that many joined their religion and were baptized. Then he continues: "There was unfortunately no priest. Initiated into everything else, they further

76

desired those sacraments which, among us, are conferred by none but a priest. Yet they understand them and desire them with the greatest eagerness. They zealously disputed among themselves whether, without the authority of the Christian pontiff, one selected out of their number might attain the character of the priesthood. It seemed likely that they would have such an election, but, to tell the truth, they had not yet done so by the time I departed" (Lupton, pp. 269 f.). Such is the uncertainty with which the humanist speaks, the friend of Erasmus, the Englishman not prone to making decisions in matters of doctrine. It follows quite naturally and logically that this early representative of Enlightenment religion was executed as a martyr for papal primacy, and in our day has been canonized as a protagonist of the papacy.

The question whether such isolated Christians as pictured by Luther and by More can, as a Christian congregation, rightfully put a man into the office of the holy ministry reveals whether a person thinks evangelically or not. There has never been an evangelical theologian who basically disagreed with Luther in such a case, not even A. Vilmar, the most "high church" among the Lutherans of last century, and certainly not Löhe. Vilmar regarded the situation put by Luther as rather fanciful, as a borderline case that could scarcely occur in real life. But should such a case actually occur, then he would agree with Luther that the congregation has the right to act as they did in Luther's story. And so Vilmar remains within the boundary drawn by the Evangelical faith. [He says:] "In situations of necessity, such as when little congregations (ecclesiolae) are cut off without contact, they can indeed have one from among them be their emergency shepherd (Nothirte). Although this is possible, it does smack of storytelling. But never may such a case be used to establish the regular way of doing things" (Die Lehre vom geistlichen Amt, p. 74).

The regular way in Vilmar as in Löhe is that shepherds are ordained by shepherds, which is also regarded as the normal thing in the Confessions of the Lutheran Church and its church orders. Here our church expressly acknowledges the ancient catholic practice. The church of the Lutheran Reformation, however, has never been in doubt regarding the possibility of the office being bestowed without the traditional ordination by an ordained servant of the Word. Herein is agreement also among all those who do not simply regard the exercise of the holy ministry as the priesthood of all believers performing its function. What makes a priest a priest is the offering of sacrifices. In the New Testamental and Evangelical sense this means the bringing of the spiritual offerings of the whole church [1 Peter 2:5]. The preaching of the Gospel and the administering of the sacraments are connected, to be sure, with such spiritual sacrifices, but they are not in themselves the functions of a priest.

6

That the great freedom of the Reformation is truly the freedom of the Gospel is shown by the fact that the Office of the Keys is given three times in the New Testament: in Matthew 16 to Peter, in John 20 to all the apostles, in Matthew 18 to the whole church. These three bestowals of the office may not be separated. One may not be selected as the chief one, and then played off against the others. To the Twelve Jesus gave the office of preaching the Gospel to every creature and making disciples of all nations by baptizing them. To them He gave the mandate at the Last Supper: "Do this in remembrance of Me." Who were the Twelve? They were the first ministers (*Amtsträger*). From them proceeds "the ministry of teaching the Gospel and administering the sacraments" [AC 5]. But they are at the same time the church, the *ekklēsia*, the representatives of God's new people of the end time.

It is therefore in fact impossible in the New Testament to separate ministry and congregation. What is said to the congregation is also said to the office of the ministry, and vice versa. The office does not stand above the congregation, but always in it. In Acts 13 Paul and Barnabas are sent out as missionaries by the congregation in Antioch. They were already sent by the Lord. What more could this congregation give to Paul with the laying on of hands than what he had already received by the direct commissioning of the risen Lord, who appointed him to his work? Nevertheless the sending is quite deliberately repeated with the laying on of hands. Office and congregation belong inseparably together.

Church history confirms this. Only where there is a vital ministerial office, working with the full authority of having been sent, only there is a living congregation. And only where there is a living congregation is there a living ministerial office. Vilmar's pessimism about the congregation can be explained by the fact that he did not yet know a living congregation. . . . [We omit a few sentences in which Dr. Sasse deplores the lack of living congregations in German Protestantism.] Of all Lutheran churches there can hardly be another in which the office of the ministry is so highly honored as in the Missouri Synod, where the congregation is so much the center of churchly thinking and activity. Office and congregation are piped together. The life of the one is also the life of the other. If the office falters, so does the congregation. If the congregation falters, so does the office.

Already for this reason the alternative "ministry or congregation?" in the 19th century was falsely put. Löhe himself saw this, by the way, as Hebart has shown in his illuminating book about him. What was lacking was the strength to draw the consequences of this recognition, and instead there was misapprehension in diagnosing what lay behind the other's position. The position taken by Missouri had nothing to do with the American propensity to do things democratically, as Mundinger has shown in his penetrating study *Government in the Missouri Synod*. After all, Walther and those like-minded with him were all antidemocrats. And Hebart has shown that no conservative political notions distorted the concept of the church for Löhe, who was never so dominated by nationalistic motives as were Bezzel and the later representatives of Neuendettelsau. On both sides there was an overemphasis on one aspect of Biblical truths which in the New Testament belong together. This happened because each party took one side of the New Testament passages as the important one, under which the other had to be subordinated.

7

Much light is thrown on the whole matter by an examination of the question of how the office of the ministry is bestowed. There is an *immediate call*. Here God calls directly without human intermediary. So it was with the apostles, prophets, and teachers. (We are not here taking into account those who were given gifts of healing and other such charismata.) Only Christ can make a man an apostle. When a man was called to replace Judas, He did it through the casting of lots. God has reserved for Himself the right of calling a person to be a prophet. Neither in the Old Testament nor in the New does a man cooperate in his being called to be a prophet. So also a teacher was regarded in the early church as being called in this way. To him was given the particular gift of expounding Scripture, which was then the Old Testament. The offices of those who were thus directly called by God belonged to the whole church. Those to whom these offices were given could exercise the functions of their office anywhere. The church, the congregation, had only to recognize them as having been given the gifts of their office—or to recognize them as false apostles, false prophets, or false teachers. This was a difficult task, which could be accomplished only through the gift of discerning the spirits.

There is also the *mediated call* for the offices of a particular congregation. These offices also are bestowed by the Lord Christ, but He does it through men. Such were the bishops and deacons, who were already there in the Pauline congregations (Phil. 1:1). They were chosen by the congregation. Similarly the presbyters, where this institution of the synagogue was maintained. It was determined by the decision of the congregation who should belong to this body of "honored ones" who sat in the first seats, the places of honor in the divine service (Matt. 23:6). Clearly there were some congregations where the arrangement was episcopal-diaconal, and others where the arrangement was presbyterial (Acts 20:17 ff.). This diversity was not something Paul thought important to set aside. Not until the Pastoral Epistles do we see them growing together into a unity. We are also not told in the New Testament who it was that elected these congregational officers. Was it the whole congregation or was it done by the "honored ones," a part of the congregation, as was the case in Rome at the time of the First Epistle of Clement—although the whole congregation was certainly involved in giving its approval.

Nothing is more misleading than to read the notions and rules of modern political or social theory into the ways things were ordered in the New Testament. The church (*ekklēsia*) is not a democracy in our sense of the term. It is not a collection of individuals, each of whom may claim the same rights. But one also dare not picture it as aristocratic. It is a body whose members are joined together in different ways and with different rights and functions. Even the body of presbyters, which was itself a unity, had different grades within it, for outstanding among them were those "who rule well . . . especially those who labor in preaching and teaching" (1 Tim. 5:17), that is, those who were also bishops. Also the laity (the Christian people) were an order, below which there were the order of the catechumens and still lower orders (*Stände*).

A person was usually placed in the orders and offices of the congregation by the laying on of hands with prayer. This laying on of hands could be done by a single person, as the apostle Paul did (2 Tim. 1:6). Or it could be done by the presbytery (1 Tim. 4:14), or by both, as was apparently the case with Timothy, or by a whole congregation through their representatives (Acts 13:3).

It is important to observe that the idea of a succession of the laying on of hands did not yet exist in the second century. The oldest succession

80

list we have is that of the church in Rome, recorded by Irenaeus. But this is not a list of successive consecrations but a list of those who occupied the office of bishop, with no attention paid to who laid hands on each one. Here also, certainly in the early days, there was considerable diversity. None of the Catholic theories regarding ordination and consecration can claim any other support from the New Testament than that with the laying on of hands and the accompanying prayer in the name of Jesus a charisma for the office is bestowed.

It should be noted that the laying on of hands, which played a large role in the church at the time of the apostles (Heb. 6:2) and was not confined to the bestowal of an office, does not belong to the essence of ordination (cf. John 20:21 ff.); that is to say, it does not have a special mandate of Christ. It is rather a usage taken over from the Old Testament, such as we find in Moses' ordination of Joshua (Num. 27:18; Deut. 34:9), and used to place into office those who were to serve the church. It is neither a sacrament, nor merely a gesture. It accompanies, and expresses the prayer, which is promised to be heard, that the Holy Spirit be present and graciously bestow His gifts. God is the One who does this, the Lord Christ, the Holy Spirit. He does this through men, whether through one, through a collegium, or through the whole congregation (Acts 20:28). This is His usual way, though He may also give such gifts directly, and with them an office.

In the light of the foregoing we may then recognize, as our Lutheran fathers did quite clearly, the impossibility of making an *essential* difference between call and ordination or even making this difference divisive of church fellowship. It is God who calls into His ministry, usually through men. The how is not the decisive thing. Whether He does it through one person, through a collegium, or through a congregation assembled in divine service, it all happens in the name of the church, the whole church, which is the body of Christ, and so it happens in the power of the Holy Spirit.

8

When one has come to recognize this, then the differences between the theological theories of the 19th century become small indeed. Then one begins to understand the glorious freedom of the Lutheran Church, which knows no law about how ministers must be placed into office (*de constituendis ministris*), because Jesus Christ did not give such a law, either directly or indirectly. When the holy ministry is received and instituted as given by the Lord, not *over* the congregation but *in* the congregation, then it becomes very large and can be received and rejoiced in as the great gift it is. Then the question how it is bestowed gives place to what is bestowed. The more or less dubious theories of its apostolic origin give place to its apostolic content. This is nothing other than what was committed to the apostles, that they should be proclaimers of the pure Gospel and servants of the sacraments instituted by Christ—this and nothing more. Herein is the apostolicity of the office of the holy ministry.

Only from this deep understanding can the spiritual office be revitalized. How unimportant then becomes all that has grown onto this office through the modern overorganization of the church; one has only to think of the church politics with which modern bishops kill their own time and that of others. Each sermon then becomes more important than all those sessions which spend their time discussing big church resolutions regarding the Bonn constitution, the atom bomb, or Goethe's 200th birthday.

Conversely: The more seriously we take the holy ministry, the more seriously we take the Christian congregation. If we did this, we would be freed from the aberration, from which our territorial churches (*Landeskirchen*) suffer so deeply, that one can draw a line around an area on the map of a city (a police district) and suppose that within that line is what the New Testament calls a congregation, and that some modern methods of caring for souls are all that is necessary to bring it to life. To think that by reporting oneself to the police station in that area as a resident one becomes a member of a Christian congregation is a notion that cannot be fitted into any Christian understanding of the church! Taking the ministry and the congregation seriously would put an end to the misunderstanding that the church taxes which the government extracts more or less painlessly are the offerings from which the church of Christ lives. It would also mean the end of the notion that what the Confessions say of church government is fulfilled by having a clever— alas, all too clever—central church bureaucracy running things not by the Word but by force (*non verbo, sed vi*).

All of this must pass away and will pass away, just as church government by princes as *summi episcopi* disappeared overnight. But the holy ministry, preaching repentance and forgiveness, and the congregation of the faithful, who in faith are justified sinners—that will remain. The future may involve forms which we today do not know about, but which the Lord of the church is preparing amid the thousandfold suffering of contemporary Christianity. He is His body's Savior even when we see only dissolution. Still true are Luther's great words about God's way in history: "By putting to death He makes alive" (*occidendo vivificat*).

This faith in what God is doing does not exclude our responsibility, but rather includes it. This means renouncing everything that is destructive of the genuine holy ministry instituted by Christ and the genuine congregation instituted by Him, everything that makes of what Christ has instituted a place for exercising our lust for power, whether clerical or congregational. The office of the holy ministry is not lord over the congregation (2 Cor. 1:24); the congregation is not lord over the office of the holy ministry (Gal. 1). Both are under Him who alone is Lord; in Him they are one.

These are just a few thoughts about church and ministry which may help you read with new awareness what God's Word has to say on this subject.

APOSTOLIC SUCCESSION

Letters to Lutheran Pastors, No. 41
April 1956

1

Apostolic succession is an ancient concept, and yet the particular implication with which it is used nowadays is, as far as I can see, a quite recent product among Christians. In 1833 appeared the first of the "Tracts for the Times," calling for a renewal of catholic thinking in the Church of England. It was a powerful summons to the Anglican clergy to ponder the responsibilities of their office. The author reminded his brother clergy that the Anglican ordination liturgy contains "the doctrine of the Apostolic Succession." He was the same John Henry Newman who 12 years later gave up this view and converted to the Roman Church.

His appeal had to be to the liturgy, since none of the confessions of the ancient church, or the Thirty-Nine Articles, contain such a doctrine. Noteworthy is also the fact that the Roman Church has no particular doctrinal article concerning the *successio apostolica*. There appears to be only one doctrinal document in which the expression is used, and that, significantly, in what the Holy Office wrote to the Catholic bishops of England in 1864 (*apostolicae successionis praerogativa*, Denzinger, 1,686).

In the Roman textbooks of dogmatics the matter itself is dealt with in the doctrine of the apostolicity of the church and in the doctrine of priestly ordination. Trent speaks of it, rather in passing, in the doctrine of the priesthood, when it says the bishops succeeded to the place of the apostles (*in apostolorum locum successerunt*, Session 23, ch. 4). In the following canons, in which the doctrines of the Reformation are rejected, there is no mention of any succession at all.

There are two places in the Interim of 1548 which approach the way in which the term is used nowadays. The Interim is not a doctrinal statement, and yet it does give a good indication of the thinking of the Catholic reform theologians at that time. Catholicity is said to be a "sign of the true church, that is, that it is universal, poured out through all places and times through the apostles and those who followed them right up to us and in continuing succession to the end of the world." Similarly the article concerning the sacrament of ordination speaks of the succession of the church: "When the bishops lay on hands and ordain to these offices, they are acting in this always continual transmission and succession of the church." [Melhausen, pp. 66, 94].

What nowadays is called apostolic succession is regarded in the Catholic churches as so self-evident that there is scarcely need to talk about it. It is quite simply given with the sacrament of priestly ordination. When the Church of England and its daughter churches (recently also certain Lutheran churches, and union churches such as that of South India) make so much of their apostolic succession, one is prompted to ponder the fact that we are most apt to speak of those virtues which we do not possess. It is hardly by chance that this overemphasis on apostolic succession emerged in a church which indeed claims to be catholic and to possess the three offices of bishop, priest, and deacon, and yet is unable to say what these offices actually are.

We would have no need of engaging the Anglicans and their unclarity (the product of the sorry history of their Reformation), if they were not continually beating on the doors of all other churches, demanding from Rome the recognition of their orders and from Protestants the receiving of their "apostolic succession." Prussia repeatedly looked with longing eyes at the Church of England, from the first king, mightily impressed by "no bishop, no king," to romantic Frederick William IV [1840—61] and his failed attempt to found a Jerusalem bishopric under the auspices of Prussia and England. The plans for this bishopric were what finally drove Newman to Rome. They contained the thought that the Church of England would help those churches "less fully organized."

In our lifetime we have seen a renewal of this friendly offer. It was made—to the dismay of all serious English theologians—by certain English bishops as Hitler's millennium was breaking upon us. In all seriousness they said to us that our struggle against Ludwig Müller and the other "German Christian" bishops was hopeless. The thing to do was for the German "bishops" to have themselves consecrated from England. That would bring everything into proper order. We were invited to consider the example of certain Nordic churches which enjoyed a good standing with the Church of England.

We will speak later about the fateful consequences for Lutheranism throughout the world which resulted when the churches of Sweden and Finland entered upon joint consecrations with the Anglicans. They should have said not only that such consecrations by the Church of England are null and void in the eyes of Rome, but that the notion that something more is given by them than is given to the ministry of Word and sacrament also runs counter to the Lutheran Reformation, according to the understanding of Article V of the Augsburg Confession.

The baleful consequences are plain for all to see in the mission fields of Africa and India. There we are now blessed with two groups of Lutheran missionaries. The one has "apostolic succession," the other does not. Both are more or less in church fellowship with a whole range of churches, but no longer with one another and no longer with whatever Lutheran Church faithful to the Confessions is still left in the world.

To what an extent this matter has become a problem in Germany can be seen by the shocking case of Friedrich Heiler, a professor of theology in the Evangelical faculty of Marburg. He had himself secretly consecrated bishop. Secretly he bestowed priestly ordination on Evangelical pastors so that they now secretly (their congregations were not informed) would be able to effect the "change" in the celebration of the Sacrament of the Altar. Were there ever before in Christ's church sacraments and ordinations at which what was given and what was received was not clearly stated, but kept secret, not done in the presence of the Christian congregation? The church governments in Germany would do well to keep a watchful eye on such surreptitious Romanizing, as well as on the open Calvinizing of the Lutheran heritage. Instead they make special laws and take measures against those who are again taking seriously the old heritage of genuine Lutheran catholicity, the only weapon against Romanizing.

2

In any attempt to understand all the talk nowadays about apostolic succession, we must begin with the fact that apostolicity is integral to the church. Therefore any church, any collection of people that claims to be church, claims apostolicity in its own way. Roman Catholic theologians are in the habit of dividing between apostolicity of origin, apostolicity of doctrine, and apostolicity of succession (*apostolicitas originis, doctrinae, successionis*). Every church claims the first two. Every church finally traces its origin back to the apostles and so to Jesus Christ Himself.

So it is nonsense to say that the Lutheran Church and the other Protestant churches came into being in the 16th century or even later, while the Roman Church goes back to Jesus and the apostles. The Eastern Church is evidence and protest enough against such an idea. Where was the papal church before there was a papacy? Whether any church has its origin in the church of the New Testament or not is simply a matter of faith. The Baptists and the Disciples of Christ make the claim that their church was *the* church at the time of the New Testament. Our Lutheran fathers never had the idea that they were founding a new church. They were of the conviction that Christ's one church was being renewed with the pure apostolic doctrine in contrast with Rome, which had fallen away from the Gospel.

These are matters of faith, and one should not try to settle them by appeals to historical proofs. How this goes may be seen in the polemics between the Anglicans and the English Roman Catholics. Both attempt to prove that they are the legitimate continuation of the medieval church in England. We Lutherans have no part to play in that sort of dispute, although it has often been suggested that we should.

To provide the proof for the identity of any historical construction is always enormously problematical. One may, for example, speak of an English nation and of a German nation that continue through the centuries. But if one looks more closely, one notices how great are also the differences. In what sense are the English people of Henry VIII's time identical with the 10 times as many English people of today? In what sense are today's German people identical with the people of Luther's time? Was it anything more than a fiction when it was thought that the Holy Roman Empire of Byzantium was living on in the empire of Charlemagne and the German empire of Otto the Great until it expired in 1806? Is there more of an identity between the Roman Church of today and the church of Peter's day than there is between the Roman Empire of the first century and the Holy Roman Empire around 1800? It has been observed that the difference between the church before Constantine and the church after Constantine is greater than the difference in the Western Church before and after the Reformation. Here the historical proofs of identity simply fail.

The apostolicity of origin, the claim that the church to which I belong is identical with the church of the apostles, is a matter of faith. The answer has to do with whether I consider the doctrine of my church to be apostolic. The claim of the Lutheran Church to be apostolic stands or falls with the claim that it has faithfully preserved the doctrine of the New Testament. For Lutherans certainly everything depends on the question: "Where today is the doctrine of the apostles?"

Naturally, every church claims to be apostolic also in the sense of the apostolicity of its doctrine. Now it is especially worth noting the enormous difficulties the Roman Church has gotten itself into through its development, especially since the Reformation. At the beginning of his work Luther could still—within the Roman Church—appeal to *sola scriptura*. Beside it there had long been the view of those who regarded tradition as an expansion of Scripture. How old and widespread this was we may observe in the Eastern Church, but it had never been made into dogma. It was first at Trent that tradition was set beside Scripture as a second equivalent source of revelation.

When this happens, when, to speak with the Smalcald Articles (II, II, 15), Scripture no longer alone sets up articles of faith, then Enthusiasm has forced an entry into the church. It pushes beyond the doctrine of the New Testament, destroys it, and abolishes the church's apostolicity. It is one of Luther's profoundest recognitions, also expressed in the Smalcald Articles (III, VIII), that Enthusiasm is engendered by scorn of the external Word, the words of Scripture read and preached. Enthusiasm leads to the religion of the natural man, fallen man who puts himself in God's place. Luther saw that this is the great heresy which the Enthusiasts, the pope, and Mohammed—the three forms of the Antichrist known to him—had in common.

All three cited the much-misunderstood words of our Lord in John 16:12–13: "I have yet many things to say to you, but you cannot bear them now. When the Spirit of truth comes, He will guide you into all the truth." These words find welcoming ears with the pope, the archbishop of Canterbury, the Quakers, the liberals, and all sorts of heretics. Not so much, however, the words which follow, the rule by which one can recognize whether it really was the Holy Spirit whom one has heard or whether it was only the spirit of man or a still worse spirit: "He will glorify Me, for He will take what is Mine and declare it to you" (v. 14), that is, interpret the Gospel of Christ ever more deeply and thus glorify Jesus.

How far things can go when this is not heeded we may see in the history of the Roman Church—Christianity's greatest tragedy. At first tradition is like a tethered balloon, more or less held by the apostolic witness. But with the declaration of two equivalent sources of revelation—Scripture and tradition—the rope is cut and the balloon sails with the wind, no one knows where. The answer came in the course of time.

By the 19th century it was so clear that the best Catholics were filled with anxiety. Neither in Scripture nor in the tradition of the first centuries can the grounds be found for any of the modern dogmas, from the Immaculate Conception of 1854 through the 1870 Vatican Council's papal dogma to the Assumption of Mary [1950]. None of these were known to the early church.

The doctrine of the Roman Church is no longer apostolic. Even in 1854 and 1870 it was still possible to claim to be reaching back to relatively old traditions, or to what were regarded as such. Passages of Scripture could be interpreted so as to be persuasive for faithful Catholics. With the dogma of 1950 this is at an end. The Assumption of Mary is a late legend, and only "conclusion theology" can produce Mary as *mediatrix* of all graces and *coredemptrix*.

At work here has been the "theory of development." This was proposed by J. H. Newman and has been avidly put to use. By the way, one can find it already in Möhler. This theory, which is supposed to justify the modern dogmas, is the product of Romanticism and of the 19th century as a whole (the obvious parallels are Darwin and Marx). The picture is that of a seed. At the beginning of the church all its doctrines were contained within the seed, and these then unfolded from century to century. Was not this the case with the doctrines of the Holy Trinity and the Person of the God-man?

To be sure, the understanding of these doctrines progressed through generations. They were, however, already there from the beginning in the apostolic witness. The New Testament declares that Jesus Christ is not a creature but the eternal Logos. The New Testament declares that Jesus Christ, true God and true man, is one Person. What unfolds in the church is the ever deeper understanding of the apostolic words. But nothing can unfold if it is not there in the apostolic words.

In Roman Catholic theology today we find such questions dealt with as, "Did Mary ever die?" Questions do arise which call for answers, such as, "What is the essence and the extent of papal infallibility?" Since Bernadette has been canonized and solemnly exalted "to the honor of the altars," can any good Catholic have doubt about the genuineness of the appearances at Lourdes? If we further probe the question of the authority of the papal teaching office, do we not reach the point where, in addition to Scripture and tradition, there appears a third source of doctrine, namely Christ's regent on earth?

We can only rejoice in all that is done in the Roman Church in honor of Scripture. In all doctrinal explanations attention is given to Scripture and tradition. Many a Protestant church could find much to learn here. But what are we to make of private revelations when they are claimed not by some unknown person but by the pope himself? If he experienced the miraculous sun of Fatima also in Rome, or had a vision of Christ, why does he not keep this to himself, which would be the proper way? Why is it proclaimed through the media to the city and to the world? Why does the believing Catholic accept the pope's every word in questions of faith and morals? Because he has tested it against Scripture and tradition? Certainly not, but because the pope has said it!

"The pope's word is God's word." This could be read during the war on the doors of the cathedral in Salzburg in a Lenten letter of the archbishop. Now Christians all know that human words can at the same time be God's words. "Do you believe that the forgiveness I declare is the forgiveness of God?" At Confession this question is put [Small Catechism V, 27]. But only the Word of God, the Word of the Gospel, the Word of the living proclamation of the apostolic message today—only this can be God's Word.

Into what airy heights does the balloon of supposed tradition float off when the line with Scripture is severed! When *sola scriptura* is left behind, left behind also are God's revelation and its authority. One can only think with horror of the fearful fate the Roman Church is readying for itself. After all, it is still Christianity's largest and most influential church. Is it still the church in which our fathers lived during the Middle Ages? Is it still an apostolic church? Has it not lost the apostolicity of doctrine? Not as though the apostolic witness had died out within it. That is still there. Otherwise Rome would be no church. Also in the Roman Church there are people who still believe in the Savior Jesus Christ as the only Mediator between God and men. Also in this church Christ is still present in the means of grace, to the extent that these are still there. Also in this church people are born again to eternal life. But there is also in this church that horror which Luther saw, the anti-Christian exaltation of man, whether in the cult of Mary or in the revering of the pope.

If we recognize this, we can do so only in the spirit of penitent self-examination. Perhaps the same disease, Christianity's mortal illness, lurks also in us and our church, ever ready to break out. How is it said by Luther at that place in the Smalcald Articles?

> In short, enthusiasm clings to Adam and his descendants from the beginning to the end of the world. It is a poison implanted and inoculated in man by the old dragon, and it is the source, strength, and

power of all heresy, including that of the papacy and Mohammedanism. Accordingly, we should and must constantly maintain that God will not deal with us except through his external Word and sacrament. Whatever is attributed to the Spirit apart from such Word and sacrament is of the devil (III, VIII, 9–10).

This is an earnest warning to every church. We cannot be discovering this heresy in other churches without earnestly asking also of ourselves, "Is it I, Lord?"

3

The doctrinal locus concerning the apostolic church has, beside the apostolicity of origin and the apostolicity of doctrine, also the apostolicity of *succession*. This is what looms most largely in Christian affairs nowadays. We must first ask what it actually is, this apostolic succession, which the Anglican churches esteem themselves as having, which the Church of Sweden believes it possesses, and which the Eastern churches and the Roman Church regard as their own possession.

In his famous *Symbolism* [English translation 1906] Möhler attempted to clarify the meaning of tradition for modern Catholicism. He found himself in remarkable agreement with Newman and his friends in England as well as with Russian thinkers such as Chomjakov. Möhler's view of tradition has been traced to contemporary philosophy and Romanticism's understanding of society as an organism. Thus J. Ranft, the dogmatician from Würzburg, in his learned work *Der Ursprung des katholischen Traditionsprinzips* (1931). Other Roman Catholic scholars agreed. (Cf. the collection in honor of the 100th anniversary of Möhler's death, *Die Eine Kirche*, ed. H. Tüchle, 1938.)

Möhler finds the law of tradition, which binds together the different generations of a people or of a religious society, in the life of all such societies.

The Divine Founder of our Church, when he constituted the community of believers as his permanent organ, had recourse to no other law than that which prevails in every department of human life. Each nation is endowed with a peculiar character, stamped on the deepest, most hidden parts of its being, which distinguishes it from all other nations and manifests its peculiarity in public and domestic life, in art and science, in short, in every relation. It is, as it were, the tutelary genius; the guiding spirit transmitted from its progenitors; the vivifying breath of the whole community (*Symbolism*, pp. 279 f.).

Just as there is a national spirit for peoples which sustains a people in its peculiar wholeness through the generations, so there is also such a spirit in religious communities. As examples of this we are given not only the Chinese, the Parsees, the Moslems, and Hellenic heathenism, but even Lutheranism:

> Lastly, let us contemplate the religious sect founded by Luther himself. The developed doctrines of his Church, consigned as they are in the symbolical books, retain, on the whole, so much of this spirit, that on the first view, they must be recognized by the observer as genuine productions of Luther (*echt lutherisch*). With a sure vital instinct (*Lebensgefühle*), the opinions of the Majorists, the Synergists and others were rejected as deadly; and, indeed (from Luther's point of view, *Geist*), as untrue, by that community whose soul, whose living principle he was; and the Church, which the Reformer of Wittenberg established, proved herself the unerring interpretess of his word (pp. 280 f.).

What revealing sentences these are! Plain for all to see is the utter distortion of Lutheranism, and so a lot of words are not called for to show that the Lutheran Church is not a religious association founded by Luther, having as its principle the spirit of Luther. What is most significant is that this way of speaking about a church is not put right even if we cross out "Luther" and substitute "Christ"; instead of what was allegedly established by the Reformer of Wittenberg, the church established by Christ; instead of the Lutheran Church as "unerring interpretess" of the words of Luther, the Roman Catholic Church as "unerring interpretess" of the words of Christ. In the tradition of doctrine and the succession of teachers there is said to be an inherent spirit at work infallibly revealing things. We hardly needed the specific references to the Chinese, Greeks, Parsees, and Moslems to recognize that such an idea is no product of the Christian faith and the witness of the apostles. Such an idea did indisputably exist throughout the ancient world, Hellenic and Asiatic, and it has certainly not died out. But what has to be decisively disputed is that the idea is a Biblical and Christian one, although there are indeed traces here and there of its influence on the *language* used in the Bible, and we may observe how later it infiltrated Christ's church and helped form the idea of the "catholic" church.

The Holy Spirit, who creates unity of faith and confession, is not the collective spirit of the Christian religious association. The church as the people of God is something completely other than the people of Mani or Mohammed. The church as the body of Christ is not an organism such

92

as a secular association, a family, a nation, or any other kind of "body." Möhler's misunderstanding, and that of the whole Romantic movement, cannot be excused by pointing to the ancient church's use of terms from ancient sociology of religion in speaking of the church of Christ. One must never forget that the church fathers came out of ancient heathenism and continued to carry some of its concepts around with them for a long time, for instance in their apologetics. The vital distinction to be made is between what is truly Biblical and what was brought into the church from that ancient heathen world. Clearly the catholicity and apostolicity of the church are taught in Holy Scripture. The same cannot be said of the way catholicity and apostolicity were understood through the centuries of the development of the Catholic Church.

We have only to look at the sentence Augustine penned to overthrow the Donatists: "When the whole world passes judgment, that judgment is sure" (*Securus iudicat orbis terrarum*). He refers to the church everywhere; the Donatists were to be found only in Africa. This is the sentence that began to shake Newman's faith in the catholicity of the Church of England. Ever and again it has deeply impressed Catholic and high-church circles. It does not come, however, from Scripture but from the religious thought of the non-Christian world, perhaps from very early forms of religion which are still alive within us or could become so. "The voice of the people is the voice of God" (*Vox populi vox Dei*. [Cf. Seneca the Elder, *Controversia*, 1, 1, 10; Homer, *Odyssey*, 3, 214 f.]). This is Stoic philosophy, and at the same time a piece of ancient wisdom—or foolishness. "My community will never agree in error" [*Haddith. Muctamad*, 458—76. Cf. Lammens, *Islam* (1968), p. 93]. Thus from Mohammed the doctrine of *ijmāʿ*, the consensus of all Moslems.

Möhler is quite right in observing that here we are dealing with doctrines which appear also outside the church. What he failed to observe is that they do not come from Holy Scripture, and indeed cannot be brought into agreement with Scripture.

How useless, indeed impossible, it is to understand the doctrine of the church from such principles is shown by the impossibility of putting into practice the well-known dictum of Vincent of Lerins. According to this dictum, that doctrine is to be regarded as catholic, and thus orthodox, "which has been believed everywhere, always, and by all" [*quod ubique, quod semper, quod ab omnibus creditum est*). Of the geographical catholicity of "everywhere" we have already spoken. It is difficult to say anything better regarding the temporal catholicity of "always," or what is often called apostolicity. Here, however, we come upon the heart of the doctrine of "apostolic succession." What is this heart? It is the conviction of all the great schools of wisdom and established religions of Asia and the Hellenistic world that in the beginning there was truth and that it was handed down in purity from generation to generation, from father to son, from master to disciples, as from hand to hand, without anything being added or taken away. The *quasi per manus tradita* ["as though passed on by hand"] which appears in the fourth session of Trent (Denzinger 783) is an age-old technical term for this.

Now how much of this can be found in Holy Scripture? In 1 Cor. 11:23 and 15:3 Paul uses the technical terms for the receiving and passing on of a tradition (*parelabon, paredōka*). (We may note in passing that this has no adverse effect on the independence of his apostleship, which he so strongly emphasizes in Galatians.) In the New Testament we do have tradition in the sense of the message of the Gospel, or some particular message, being faithfully kept and handed on (1 Tim. 6:20), without addition or subtraction (Rev. 22:18–19). This "tradition," however, whether it be the oral proclamation of the apostles or whether it was already written down, has nothing to do with a tradition which was later placed in opposition to Scripture. The apostolic witness cannot be divided into what was preached and what was written down. These are one and the same. The authentic doctrinal tradition of the church in the sense of the New Testament is never anything else than the living transmission of this witness in preaching and instruction. It can never be an independent source of revelation. Authentic apostolic succession, then, is always and only the succession of doctrine. It may be known by its identity with the witness of the apostles in the New Testament. In this way the content of what is proclaimed by any and every church is to be weighed.

There is indeed also a succession of teachers who have faithfully proclaimed the apostolic message. But who these surely are only God knows, just as He alone "knows those who are His," who are truly His church [2 Tim. 2:19].To set down lists of such succession is an understandable desire. It is a human desire which in the ancient world produced lists of teachers, chains of transmitters of a tradition, in many schools and religions. It was therefore a piece of ancient non-Christian religion that penetrated into the church with the setting up of lists of those who held office and were transmitters of tradition. People sought in human books what is written only in the books of God.

94

4

The problem with these lists of succession may be illustrated by two examples, touching the Old and the New Testament. How rabbinic Judaism understood the handing down of what was taught in the Old Testament is shown by the chain of tradition with which the Mishna tractate *Pirqe Abot* ("Sayings of the Fathers") begins. "Moses received the Torah from Sinai and transmitted it to Joshua, Joshua to the elders, the elders to the prophets, and the prophets transmitted it to the men of the Great Synagogue." The line then continues through Simon the Just (ca. 300 B.C. or a century later) to the rabbis of the later period. We need not enter upon the question whether the Great Synagogue ever actually existed or whether it was a fiction developed out of Nehemiah 8—10. It is enough to consider the inclusion of the prophets in the list of those who transmitted the Torah to recognize the fiction. This artificial construction was intended to show the transmission of divine truth through the generations. The history of Old Testament revelation is pressed into a scheme whose origin is not Biblical and which cannot be brought into agreement with the Biblical record.

Our second example is the understanding of New Testament revelation to be found in 1 Clement. There we read in chapter 42:

> The apostles for our sake were given the Gospel as proclaimed to them by the Lord Jesus Christ. Jesus the Christ was sent from God. Christ, therefore, is from God and the apostles from Christ. . . . When they had received their instructions, having been filled with certainty by the resurrection of our Lord Jesus Christ and strengthened by the Word of God, they went out full of confidence in the Holy Spirit, proclaiming the Gospel that the kingdom of God was about to come. Through the country and the towns they preached, and appointed their firstfruits, after testing them by the Spirit, to be bishops and deacons of those who would believe. Nor was this any new thing, for a long time ago there was mention of bishops and deacons in Scripture. For there is somewhere in Scripture a passage which says, "I will appoint their bishops in righteousness and their deacons in peace."

Where is this written? Nowhere. The author probably had in mind Is. 60:17, where the Septuagint (literally translated) has, "I will give your rulers (*archontas*) in peace and your overseers (*episkopous*) in righteousness." Do we have here only a lapse of memory, or is it a "spiritual" interpretation of the passage? In that case, though, it should somehow be indicated. As the text stands in 1 Clement it is a spurious quotation.

There is much to ponder in the fact that such a falsification or whatever one may call it (perhaps our norms are not applicable to an earlier time) occurs in the first document of the Roman Church, near the end of the first century. The document sets up as a law that those who bear churchly office are undeposable without evidence against them, and this is imposed upon another church with the demand of obedience [59:1] and the claim to be giving a decision given by the Holy Spirit [63:2]. This was at a time when there was not yet a monarchic episcopate in Rome, let alone a papacy. Clement was one of the bishops in Rome, and we learn from the Shepherd of Hermas that he had the responsibility of correspondence with congregations elsewhere [Vis. II, 4, 3]. What he gives out as a binding decision has as its basis a falsification. Where this all leads to we may see in its fruition in the *Donation of Constantine* and the *Pseudo-Isidorian Decretals*. We here observe the first instance of that viewpoint which Cardinal Manning summed up in connection with Vatican I and its undemonstrable and untrue historical assertions about the place of the Roman bishops in the ancient church: "Dogma must prevail over history" [*Vatican Council* (1969), pp. 125 ff.].

Quite apart from the problem of the spurious quotation, we have to ask, "What is the meaning of the way history is pictured in Clement?" We find a mixture of truth and fantasy. Revelation does indeed have a chain of succession. The Father sends the Son, the Son the apostles. The apostles hand their commission (*Auftrag*) on to those who bear office (*die Amtsträger*) in the church. That is Biblical. "As the Father has sent Me, even so I send you" [John 20:21]. And the commission to proclaim the Gospel to every creature, even to the ends of the earth and until "the close of the age," was in fact given the apostles by their Lord. And of this we are told in Holy Scripture, that the apostles appointed office-bearers, both to help them and to take their place. Thus Paul put Timothy in office. According to Acts 14:23 Barnabas and Paul "appointed elders" for the mission congregations in southern Asia Minor. This historical fact was then dogmatically simplified in 1 Clement, as also by such writers of the second century as Irenaeus and Tertullian, yes, by the whole church of that time.

There is first the fact that it was not always the Twelve who founded and organized the churches, yes, not even apostles in the real meaning of the word. Indeed the greatest of the ancient churches, Antioch and Rome, were founded by unknown Christians. It is simply historically not the case that Peter and Paul were the *founders* of the church in Rome, as Irenaeus claims at the beginning of his list of Roman bishops.

It is further simply not the case that the office of the ministry [*das geistliche Amt*] always arose in the same way, namely by being received from the apostles. The Didache (15:1) gives admonition to congregations as to what to do in case there are no wandering apostles, prophets, or teachers among them:

> Elect therefore for yourselves bishops and deacons worthy of the Lord, men mild and not greedy for money, truthful, men who have been tested. They do the same service for you as the prophets and teachers. Therefore do not think less of them, for they are the honorable ones among you, along with the prophets and teachers.

What was always at first manifold is later brought into unified forms. This may be observed from the beginning of the church's history (for instance in the liturgy), and it is the case also with polity. It is the simplifying, dogmatical view which leads to such simplified constructions of history as we saw in Judaism's scheme of succession in the "Sayings of the Fathers" and in its counterpart in what Clement of Rome did for early Christianity.

5

It is well known how the great struggle against the Gnostic sects, which the church had to carry on in the second century, brought toward victory the idea of the apostolic succession of bishops and thereby created the Catholic office of bishop. From the standpoint of the Reformation we may regret that in this struggle the church was not content to trust its defense to the Rule of Faith (the early form of the Apostles' Creed) and to Holy Scripture. However, we must not forget that it was not so easy to stand by *sola scriptura* at a time when the canon of the New Testament was not yet in existence and when Holy Scripture was the Old Testament. Our New Testament had not yet emerged from the various writings which claimed to include the genuine apostolic witness. We need to consider what it meant in the year 180 for the martyrs of Scillium in North Africa that they were able to recognize the Pauline Epistles only as worthy documents but not yet as Holy Scripture [Owen, *Some Authentic Acts of the Early Martyrs* (1927), p. 72]. At that time it was not possible to draw Scriptural proof from the Epistle to the Romans. We must consider this situation of the church in order to understand what weight was then attached to the "apostolic" office of the bishops as guardians of the pure doctrine.

To explore the problem of the oldest succession lists, we turn to the work of Erich Caspar, the great historian of the papacy, whose lifework remained unfinished. From the *Schriften der Königsberger Gelehrten Gesellschaft* (1926) we have his *Die älteste Römische Bischofsliste*. Although much has been said in criticism of details of this work, its essential result remains, namely that the names Irenaeus gives in the list of bishops (*Adv. haer.* III, 3, 3) are genuine.

As Hegesippus traveled among the churches of the East and the West, he made lists of successions. He operated according to a dogmatic viewpoint which had the false presupposition that one could prove the transmission of the pure doctrine by the succession of the bishops, but his researches have given us highly valuable historical material [Eusebius, *Historia ecclesiastica* IV, 22, 1–3].

The Roman list which Irenaeus brings up to his time has nothing but authentic names. Its age and authenticity are evidenced by the fact that, in contrast with the current official list of popes, Peter does not appear as the first Roman bishop. Peter and Paul are presented as the founders of the church in Rome. They are said to have committed the episcopate to Linus. The whole following list with its numbering of the third, sixth, and ninth bishops is constructed on the presupposition that Linus was the first bishop, and that Peter and Paul put him in this office. In Rome in the third century Peter and Paul were still always named together as of equal rank.

It is clear from 1 Clement, as also from Ignatius' Epistle to the Romans, that at the beginning of the second century in Rome there was still no monarchic bishop, but rather a college of bishops. It would appear that it was the incursion of the great Gnostic sects into Rome which produced the need for a unified government of the church by one bishop. Pius, the brother of the author of the Shepherd of Hermas, seems to have been the first monarchic bishop in the chief city of the world.

Also here the rule proves true that things moved from East to West, not only the Gospel but also church institutions. Already in the Revelation to John we see that toward the end of the first century every church in the East had its own bishop ("To the angel of the church in . . . write . . . "). What then were Linus, Anacletus, Clement, Evaristus, Alexander, Sixtus, [Telesphorus], and Hyginus, who appear in the list prior to Pius? They were, as Harnack already saw, obviously outstanding members of the college of bishops, men who were renowned as teachers of the church. The list, we must judge, indeed has nothing but genuine names, and yet it is an artificial construction, similar to the succession list in the Mishna tractate.

And what was the list intended to prove? Nothing except that in Rome there was a tradition of doctrine, that the apostolic message was faithfully handed on from generation to generation. The point of the list is that there was a succession of teachers and therefore of doctrine. Others could have been named, for all these "bishops" had colleagues associated with them. These names may have been chosen because of the reputation of these men, but a "succession" in a strictly historical sense it was not. Without historical foundation are also the "years of reign" with which they were later supplied. There is no solid evidence for dates until the middle of the [second] century.

6

The greatest difference between the old Roman list of bishops and other lists of bishops on the one hand and what is today understood by "apostolic succession" on the other hand is the following. These lists, such as the official Roman list of popes, and the list of the archbishops of Canterbury or of Cologne, give the names of the incumbents of a particular bishop's seat, one after the other. They do not speak, and do not intend to speak, of a succession of *consecrations*. The incumbent of a bishop's seat is not consecrated by his predecessor. Succession of office must be strictly differentiated from succession of consecration. This latter only gradually began to play a part in the church. Yet today this is the idea of apostolic succession that is so insisted on: A bishop receives his consecration from another bishop, whose consecration goes back to other bishops, right back to the first bishops who were consecrated by the apostles.

How historical is this succession? In later times it can certainly be demonstrated or accepted with confidence, for after the year 200 the old usage stood firm that a bishop was chosen by the clergy and people of his church but that he could receive consecration only from one or (very soon) several bishops. [A presbyter might consecrate a bishop (*Canons of Hippolytus* II, 10).] It also became settled practice that only a bishop could ordain presbyters and deacons [Council of Ancyra, Canon 13], as also that ordination was done with the laying on of hands. But does this tell us that all consecrations go back to the apostles? Timothy was ordained by Paul with the laying on of hands (2 Tim. 1:6). In 1 Tim. 3 and 5 he was given instruction for appointing bishops, deacons, and widows (deaconesses), where the laying on of hands is explicitly mentioned. But were bishops everywhere ordained in this way? How were things done in Rome in Clement's day? We do not know.

The historian may regret a gap in our knowledge of what went on, but for one who believes Scripture to be God's Word there is a deeper meaning in the fact that we nowhere have a mandate of our Lord to carry out an ordination, let alone instructions as to how it should be done. We have the mandate to baptize. We have the mandate to repeat the Lord's Supper, and there is the institution of the Office of the Keys. This last, we do well to note, in threefold form: Matt. 16 to Peter, Matt. 18 to the assembled congregation, and John 20 to the Twelve (more precisely the disciples who were gathered on the evening of Easter Day). But no one has been able to show when Jesus ordained the Twelve. The Catholic churches have to resort to the command to repeat the Lord's Supper. With the words "This do in remembrance of Me" Jesus is said to have ordained the apostles to be priests.

It cannot be without significance that we hear of no laying on of hands. Jesus laid His hands on children and on the sick, but not on the Twelve. Where we might most expect it, when He gives them the Office of the Keys, there at John 20:21 ff. we read: "Jesus said to them again, 'Peace be with you. As the Father has sent Me, even so I send you.' And when He had said this, He breathed on them, and said to them, 'Receive the Holy Spirit. . . .' " One almost gets the impression that here, as whenever He sent out the apostles, Jesus intentionally avoided the laying on of hands. Such an avoidance may have been due to the fact that ordination by laying on of hands was rabbinical usage. That is how a rabbi ordained his disciples. Pondering what Jesus said against the scribes in Matt. 23 may suggest why Jesus did not follow their usage. Does He not say that among those that are His the title "rabbi" is not to be used, "for you have one Teacher (*didaskalos*), and you are all brethren" (v. 8)?

This did not prevent the title "teacher" from being used in the church for the great office of expounding Holy Scripture, at first the Old Testament. This office, along with that of the apostles and prophets, was foundational in the beginnings of the church, recognized not only in a particular congregation but throughout the church. And, after all, the title "teacher" was not directly prohibited by the words of our Lord. (Cf. also "master" (kathēgētēs, v. 10.)

However that may have been, it was certainly bad that, under the pressure of age-old Eastern custom, and against the express will of

Jesus, the church again took up the title "father" in place of "teacher" and first of all addressed the bishop thus (*pappas, papa,* cf. *abbas* in monasticism). (Cyprian of Carthage was still addressed thus; today the title is restricted to the bishop of Rome and the patriarch of Alexandria.)

The suggestion that Jesus was acting in deliberate contrast and opposition to the rabbis when He avoided the laying on of hands in what we might call ordination is strengthened by the noteworthy fact that the rabbis no longer followed the usage of the laying on of hands when in the second century it had become a characteristic of Christian ordination. So the laying on of hands is an early usage in the church (Heb. 6:2), with an Old Testament background (Moses laid his hands on Joshua, Deut. 34:9; cf. Num. 27:18), but it cannot be said to be something that Christ commanded us to do, let alone be called a sacrament. It was a way of bestowing a blessing, and that it certainly did.

It is also clearly not something that was reserved to the holder of a particular office. Beside the laying on of hands done by the apostles was also that done by the elders. Elders were men of special standing, not incumbents of a specific office. Thus it was in the synagogue, in the church of Jerusalem, in the Pauline congregations, and still so in Rome at the time of Clement. Elders were elected by the congregation as "honored ones," as *prōtokathedritai* ("having the first seats"), as they are still called in the Shepherd of Hermas [Vis. III, 9, 7; cf. 1 Clement 1:3; 21:6]. Because of their age, because of what they had done for the congregation, or for some other reason, they occupied the first places in the divine service. They represented the congregation. From among them the bishops were chosen, the group of officers who led the congregation, in particular to perform the office of preaching the Word or of saying the liturgical prayers, especially during the Eucharist. They did what was otherwise reserved to the prophets. Elders who then also performed such offices were to be "considered worthy of double honor, especially those who labor in preaching and teaching." What is said in 1 Tim. 5:17 matches perfectly what is said of the situation in Rome in 1 Clement. The elders as representatives of the congregation participated in the ordination of Timothy. They laid their hands on him (1 Tim. 4:14), as also did the apostle [2 Tim. 1:6].

How free was the usage of the laying on of hands in the early church we may see from the noteworthy passage Acts 13: 1–3, where the church ordains an apostle. Here in Antioch we find prophets and teachers officiating, among them Barnabas (from the sound of the words a prophet) and Paul (the schooled scribe) as "teacher," that is, as one who expounds the Scriptures. During the liturgy the Holy Spirit by way of prophetic statement (as in the case of Timothy) instructs them to send out Barnabas and Paul on a special mission. "Then after fasting and praying they laid their hands on them and sent them off" (v. 3). In the early church there are more examples of a teacher becoming a missionary. There was Pantaenus, who gave up the office of teacher in Alexandria in order to go as a missionary to "India" [Eusebius, *Historia ecclesiastica* V, 10, 2].

Who laid on hands here? The congregation, perhaps through its elders. I have never been able to understand how learned Catholics, such as Tixeront in his well-known work on ordination [*Holy Orders (1928)*, p. 142] can read Acts 13:3 in such a way that the laying on of hands by the congregation could be taken as little more than a sort of godspeed for a good journey. The problem here is that the later Roman Catholic idea of ordination is being read back into a time when it had not as yet developed, or to say the least, into a time when there was greater diversity of forms in the life of the church. One has only to study such forms as they have survived on the fringes of ancient Christianity, in Ethiopia or in old Ireland, to see how at the beginning there was always diversity, which under the influence of the great metropolitan centers was reduced to unified forms.

7

What emerges from the foregoing? Here so much could only be pointed to, and yet what help have we found for dealing with the problem of the "apostolic succession" today? From a doctrinal point of view it can only be seen as a soap bubble, on which no church can be built. The Roman Church has the wisdom to put the whole matter in its doctrine of the priesthood. Rome knows that apostolic succession, in the double sense of a sequence of bishops and a succession of consecrations, has never guaranteed what the ancient church wished to have guaranteed, namely purity of doctrine, the apostolicity of the church. Rome also knows how many bishops, consecrated with every proper rite, have fallen away in persecutions or into heresy. The church in the East knows this too.

Bishop Lilje, then, is crashing through open doors when he charges that it is heresy to affirm that the apostolic succession guarantees pure doctrine. Rome does not affirm this. For Rome the purity of the doctrine, the apostolicity of the church, is guaranteed by the office of Christ's infallible vicar as successor of the "Prince of the Apostles." The significance of the succession of consecrations/ordinations for Rome is simply and only that which is expressed in the liturgy of ordination to the priesthood: the power to offer the sacrifice of the Mass for the living and the dead (*potestas ordinis*) and the power of the Office of the Keys (*potestas iurisdictionis*). The silken thread upon which the Roman doctrine of office hangs is the notion that when our Lord said: "Do this in remembrance of Me," He wanted to ordain the apostles to be priests. If these words are to be understood differently, namely in the sense that the Twelve here as in other passages are the representatives of God's people as a whole, then the entire special priesthood simply collapses. The New Testament knows that in the new covenant there is only one high priest, Jesus Christ, and the priestly people of God, whose members are kings and priests.

If the Reformers, indeed also the fathers of the Reformed churches, including the Anglican, saw one thing clearly, it is that it is quite untenable to hold this interpretation of our Lord's bidding that His Supper be repeated. In addition Matt. 18:18 makes it clear that the Keys are not the sole prerogative of the clergy. Evidence of their belonging to the whole church may be found in the early church and for a long time thereafter. There is the lovely story related by Melanchthon in the Treatise on the Power and Primacy of the Pope (67 f.), ascribed to Augustine and to be found also in Gratian's *Decretum*, where it appears as an illustration for a point of canon law. Two shipwrecked Christians were together in a boat. One was a catechumen. Him the other baptized, and then by him was absolved. The view of the Lutheran Confessions that the keys have been given to the whole church is in harmony with Scripture and the ancient church.

If one accepts the Roman view, then the apostolic succession makes some sense: The power to make the sacrifice of the Mass and the power to absolve is bestowed. If one does not accept this view, then there is no apostolic succession. Leo XIII was then quite right in declaring Anglican orders to be null and void, because their form, that is, the words of ordination, was invalid and because the right intention was lacking.

The words of ordination of the Anglican ritual are indeed ambiguous. One must probably be an Anglican in order not to see that they are therefore impossible.

> Receive the Holy Ghost for the office and work of a Priest in the Church
> of God, now committed unto thee by the imposition of our hands.
> Whose sins thou dost forgive, they are forgiven; and whose sins thou

dost retain, they are retained. And be thou a faithful dispenser of the Word of God, and of his holy sacraments.

These words can mean ordination to the Gospel office of proclaiming the Word and administering the sacraments. "Priest" then means presbyter, in the general sense which was the usage for a long time in North Germany and is still the usage in Scandinavia, where the parson is called "priest." This is the way the formula is understood by evangelically minded Anglicans. Among the High Church and Anglo-Catholics, however, "priest" means *sacerdos*, one who offers sacrifice at the consecration in Holy Communion. As to right intention, what the ordaining bishop may be thinking he is doing is left up to him. This is also the case with what is meant by the formula for consecrating a bishop, whose office is said to be "the office and work of a Bishop in the Church of God." What is essential to this office is not said.

This way of doing things is characteristic of Anglicanism. We may look for its roots in the character of the English people, as well as in the inexpressibly sad story of the English Reformation, which was at first an event of national politics rather than a religious event. This is not to deny all that has been and is great in this church; there is much for us Lutherans to learn from it. Its "apostolic succession" we cannot, however, acknowledge; it is an empty form.

For us there are different grounds than those of Rome for rejecting Anglican "apostolic succession." For us the matter is not decided by whether the consecrating of Archbishop [Matthew] Parker [in 1559] was adequately done: Two bishops with Roman Catholic consecration (but without office), plus two Reformed bishops participated. This is also not the direction of the Roman arguments against the validity of Anglican orders. As we have seen, these attach to the faulty formula of ordination and the lack of the intention to make the one ordained into a priest in the Roman Catholic sense. Against these considerations the laying on of hands, be it ever so canonical, is of no avail. When our Anglican friends would make us in our "less fully organized churches" into successors of the apostles by their laying on of hands, we will have to teach them that the genuine succession of the apostles is that which lives by the pure proclamation of the Gospel and celebration of the sacraments, and not by the myth of an unbroken chain of consecrations going all the way back to the apostles.

8

Not to see this clearly is for Lutherans a grievous failure. Of the offered "apostolic succession," we must ask what is its nature and what are the consequences of accepting such an ecclesiastical myth. The sooner the answers, the better. We may recall the answer given by Archbishop Söderblom at the World Conference for Faith and Order at Lausanne in 1927. Whatever else may be said of his limitations, it was surely a piece of his Lutheran heritage which came to sober expression when he said that the Church of Sweden has preserved the apostolic succession together with other things inherited from the ancient church, but that such a succession is according to Lutheran doctrine an adiaphoron. This he did quite unforgettably. He threw aside the printed text of what he had intended to say, for he felt compelled to speak even more clearly. For that all Lutherans were grateful.

If one looks more closely at the Swedish succession, it is really much better than the Anglican one. The critical link was a man who had just been consecrated by the pope himself in Rome, or, as Luther might say, the succession was received directly from the Roman Antichrist. But just this circumstance shows what nonsense it is to regard succession as more than time-honored custom and to consider it as theologically necessary or important. As an old ecclesiastical form, as an adiaphoron, it can be borne with that humor with which Söderblom carried his bishop's staff. Once, during a visitation, he realized that he had forgotten to pack it. It was quickly replaced by one cut from a birch tree. Is it possible for a Swedish Lutheran seriously to suppose that a pope who rejected the doctrine of the Lutheran Reformation as heresy could be the one to guarantee that the Church of Sweden has indeed true bishops and pastors?

Yet even there the old, healthy view of succession, the view in harmony with the Lutheran Confessions, seems to be losing ground in influential circles. In the official statement about itself in the handbook of the Lutheran World Federation, *The Lutheran Churches of the World*, ed. A. R. Wentz (1952), p. 171, we read that the Church of Sweden accepted the Unaltered Augsburg Confession in 1593 and that since 1686 the Book of Concord is the church's confession. Then on p. 174 we read: "Sweden's apostolic succession has opened the way for intercommunion with the Church of England," an intercommunion that has meanwhile been raised by both parties to the level of church law.

About the consequences of all this for Lutheranism around the world more than enough has already been said in these letters. We can only ask why others did not raise their voices while there was still time. Where was the voice of the bishops of Norway and of Denmark? Where was the voice of the Lutheran churches of Germany and of America? Where was the voice of the Lutheran missions? They looked on complacently when Lutheran bishops were consecrated with the assistance of Anglican bishops and archbishops. They were silent when it was up to them to raise their voices in warning; they owed this brotherly service to the Lutheran churches of the world. The old Archbishop Johannson of Finland was the first to see where this path would lead. His voice died away unheard.

We all reassured ourselves at first with the fact that the "apostolic succession" is an adiaphoron—and that it is, if it is understood in the Lutheran manner as simply a form from the ancient church. But there comes a time when an adiaphoron ceases to be an adiaphoron. This is said with all necessary clarity in Article X of the Formula of Concord. This article was a beacon and banner for us in the church struggle in Germany, and we were privileged to experience that it is still a weapon with which one can fight for the church of God. "In a case of confession or scandal nothing is an adiaphoron." Where the pure doctrine of the Gospel is at stake, there toleration of adiaphora ceases. There it is the duty of "the entire community of God . . . and especially the ministers of the Word as the leaders of the community . . . to confess openly, not only by words but also through their deeds and actions . . . " (Formula of Concord, Solid Declaration, X, 10).

We are not in a position to tell the Lutherans in Sweden who hold to the old heritage of their church (it is a truly great heritage) what they should do in order to preserve the pure Gospel of justification by faith alone and the pure administration of the sacraments, to which pure proclamation about the sacraments also belongs. We can pray for them. What we cannot do is acknowledge the Church of Sweden as a church of the Unaltered Augsburg Confession when it has altar fellowship with Anglicans and has Anglican bishops, who reject "by faith alone," participate in the consecration of Swedish bishops. The same must be said of other Lutheran churches when they put themselves into a similar situation.

Here the Lutheran World Federation would have a great task, the task of saying clearly what the Lutheran Confessions still mean for our day and wherein the true unity of the church resides. But can we expect anything else from it than that it simply offers justification for what has already been happening? Can we expect that it will commit suicide? It is at the outset committed to the principle that churches which are in church fellowship with the Reformed and the Anglicans are to be recognized as churches of the Unaltered Augsburg Confession, in spite of the latter's Articles VII and X, not to speak of the Formula of Concord.

The witness of the Lutheran Confessions will then have to be heard outside the Lutheran World Federation. May this happen only in humility and love! However conscious we may be of our poverty and weakness, this is the great service that is ours to do for those who have lost the confession of the Lutheran Reformation or are in danger of losing it. It is the task of those whose ordination to the Lutheran ministry gave them the authentic apostolic succession. This is no mysterious something that rests on a myth of consecrations. Rather it consists in the clear commission which our Lord gave to His whole church, to proclaim the pure apostolic doctrine and administer the sacraments according to the Gospel.

That is the great responsibility which today is given to the Lutheran pastor. It cannot be taken from him by any bishop, any church government, or any ecumenical organization. We may and can confess, also if those remain silent who are in the first instance called to do this. In faithful confession lives the whole glory of our office, even when this glory is hidden under the cross.

Last Things: Church and Antichrist

Letters to Lutheran Pastors, No. 24
March 1952

1

A few years ago, in the time of Germany's collapse, it was reported of a German pastor that he boasted of preaching only on the Revelation of St. John. Probably his poor congregation soon made it clear to him that that would not do. Yet, in his way, he was attempting to make good what had been neglected by the church and by us pastors: *eschatological proclamation.*

In our day the Biblical doctrine of the Last Things has come alive for us as a gift given in the midst of what the church has had to endure. At the beginning of this century a complacent church regarded the Last Things as an element of the first Christian proclamation which more or less belonged only to that first period, a form of the Gospel which was for us of only historical interest. Or, alternatively, it was thought of as something that might be of significance for the future, at the end of our lives, or at the end of the world, something we needed to study only in preparation for such an end. That there is for the church no more vitally relevant doctrine than that of the Last Things was brought home to Christians in Europe by all they were called upon to endure. It was not quite the same for Christians in other parts of the world, although in America some first indications can be observed of a new interest in eschatology.

There was perhaps some dark foreshadowing of what was to come when, at the beginning of the century, historical theology again discovered the eschatological character of the Gospel—much to the discomfort of the "systematic" theologians and the representatives of practical theology. No one can tell us, who have endured the judgments of God's wrath, that the fearful pictures of apocalyptic tribulation shown us in

Holy Scripture are but the product of Eastern fantasy. We can no longer read these passages the way they were expounded in earlier centuries. The old expositions seem like the work of a connoisseur who stands before some old paintings as if he had all the time in the world, and expounds what he finds so enchanting about them. He is quite at peace with himself and his expert knowledge—or his expert ignorance. The paintings mean absolutely nothing decisive for his existence.

For us these are realities of which we have had some experience. We are like those people in the East for whom Mereshkovski speaks in the introduction to *The Brothers Karamazov* (Munich, 1921).

> They are like men who stand upon some height and looking over the heads of those around them see what is coming upon them, what at the moment is not yet seen by the multitude below. Thus have we, beyond all the coming centuries and whatever could possibly happen, caught a glimpse of the end of the world's history. . . . We may indeed be the weakest of the weak. Our "power is made perfect in weakness." Our strength is in this, that we cannot be won over by any seductions of the most mighty of all devils, by any seductions of the everlasting "normality" of unending "progress." We cannot be bought by any averaged philosophy that is neither hot nor cold. Our faith is set on the end; we see the end; we long for the end. . . . In our eyes there is an expression which never was before in the eyes of men. In our hearts there is a feeling that has not been felt by men for 19 centuries, not since the vision was seen by that lonely exile on the island that is called Patmos: "The Spirit and the Bride say, 'Come.' And let him who hears say, 'Come.' . . . He who testifies to these things says, 'Surely I am coming soon.' Amen. Come, Lord Jesus!"

It is by living the Last Things that we are given a new understanding of the fact, and why it is so, that always involved in the Gospel and the proclamation of the Gospel are the Last Things, the end, Christ's return. There is preaching of the Gospel in the world because we are in the world's evening (Matt. 24:14). The reddening dawn of the daybreak of the kingdom of God is signaled by the lame walking, the blind seeing, that "lepers are cleansed and the deaf hear." Finally the nearness of the kingdom of God is signaled by the fact that "the poor have good news preached to them" [Matt. 11:5]. All preaching is preaching of the Last Things when it is preaching of the Gospel. And no preaching is preaching of the Last Things if it is not preaching of the pure Gospel— even if it were the exposition of nothing else but the Revelation of St. John and the other eschatological texts of Holy Scripture. How can anyone proclaim the Lord's death without a thought of His coming again?

How can the word "justification" come from our mouths without a thought of His coming again to judge the living and the dead? How can one say "Amen" at the end of the sermon without thinking of that great Amen at the end of the Bible: "Amen. Come, Lord Jesus"?

2

In the light of the foregoing we shall take up a single part of eschatology, a not unimportant part, *the doctrine of the Antichrist.* In dogmatics it appears, because of its nature, in two places, in the doctrine of the Last Things and in the doctrine of the church. Yet both belong together, for the doctrine of the church, when seen clearly, that is, seen in the light of God's Word, is actually only a part of eschatology. There is church only at the end of the world (1 Cor. 10:11). "In these last days," according to Heb. 1:2, "He [the Father] has spoken to us by a Son." At the end of the world the Son calls the faithful from among all nations to the true people of God, the church. All that happens in the church is fulfillment of the prophecies of the end, for example the whole activity of the Holy Spirit (Acts 2:16 ff.; Joel 2:28 ff.). The sacraments of Baptism and the Lord's Supper anticipate what happens at the end and in eternity (Rom. 6:2 ff.; 1 Cor. 11:26; John 6:54). So also Holy Absolution and the justification of the sinner anticipate what happens on the Day of Judgment. Even the liturgy on Sunday is an anticipation of the liturgy of heaven (Rev. 4), as every Sunday celebrated as "the Lord's day" anticipates the Parousia (cf. the expression "the day of the Lord," Amos 5:18). Only from this vantage point is it possible to understand the church of the New Testament and its hope anchored in the end.

The first Christians were not Adventists. Had they been, they would not have survived the Parousia's delay. In fact, the early Christian "Adventists" did fall from the faith (2 Peter 3:3 ff.). Nor were the first Christians Catholics, for whom institutionalization of the church becomes a substitute for the kingdom which has failed to come. Nor were they like some modern Protestants, for whom the kingdom of God becomes a kingdom of this world in social ethics and religiosity. Rather they lived in the great actuality of the Last Things, in the church of the living God. They were not a religious association with certain eschatological convictions. They were the holy people of the end time, the saints, who still lived in this world but no longer belonged to it. While for modern Christians, whether Catholic or Protestant, it might only be a matter of pictures and parables, for them it was a reality they actually lived when they designated themselves the people of God, the body of Christ, the temple of the Holy Spirit.

To the reality of the church, however, belongs the reality of the Antichrist. "Children, it is the last hour; and as you have heard that Antichrist is coming, so now many antichrists have come; therefore we know that it is the last hour" (1 John 2:18). Because the church lives at the end time of the world, therefore the prophecy of the coming Antichrist is being fulfilled. And because the prophecy of the Antichrist is being fulfilled, the church knows that it is the last time. So the appearance of the Antichrist must run through the whole history of the church. The Antichrist is always coming, and he is already here. Similarly in Paul, who does not use the word "Antichrist," "the man of lawlessness . . . the son of perdition, who opposes and exalts himself . . . " is coming, but in such a way that "the mystery of lawlessness is already at work." But it will only then be fully revealed when "in his time" he comes "by the activity of Satan . . . with all power and with pretended signs and wonders" (2 Thess. 2:3 ff.).

Both apostles agree that the Antichrist is on his way, insofar as his appearance belongs to the end time. Both see him active in the present and in the future. While Paul looks more to the future, John focuses more on the present. This matches what they say elsewhere about eschatology. Their unity is not diminished by whether the emphasis is on the present or on the future in an end time that embraces both the present and the future. We must not bend Paul to John or John to Paul. Rather we must recognize how in them both we have the one harmonious doctrine of the Antichrist.

We may not use our notions of time to make measurements of the last time as we are told of it in Scripture (2 Peter 3:3–9). There seems to be a contradiction between the fact that the Lord is coming soon and that 19 centuries have now passed since this was proclaimed. This we simply accept, as we also do the fact that at the time of John it was already "the last hour," in which the Antichrist was in the world, and that the time of his being revealed still lies ahead.

One cannot weaken this apparent contradiction by explaining it away in terms of a development from the comparatively harmless antichrists of the early time to the anti-Christianity which comes to consummation at the Parousia. First of all, Holy Scripture does not know our concept of development; it was first read into Scripture by the evolutionistic 19th century. Furthermore, what John tells of anti-Christianity is no less satanic, no less dangerous, than what Paul sees. Both

111

derive from the same source: the devil. Both have the same goal: to cast Jesus Christ from His throne and to destroy His true church. Both fight with the same weapons: the power of the lie, and deceptions which seduce to falling away from the true God (1 John 2:22 ff.; 2 John 7; 2 Thess. 2:3, 9 ff.). The difference is only in the outward appearance. In John the Antichrist appears in the shape of many men who are called antichrists, in Paul in the shape of "the man of lawlessness." What we are told of is the same, whether in one form of appearance or the other.

The language in 2 Thess. 2:3 is clearly picturesque and apocalyptic. That he "takes his seat in the temple of God" is apocalyptic picture language ever since the desecration of the temple by Antiochus Epiphanes, as seen by Daniel. Similarly, that Christ "will slay him with the breath of His mouth" belongs to the picture language of the Messianic hope in the prophets (compare 2 Thess. 2:8 with Is. 11:4 and Rev. 19:15, 20).

Hence it must remain an open question whether the prophecy of "the man of lawlessness" will be fulfilled in the form of one individual man. Elert has a telling comment on the apocalyptic visions in the Bible: "Not the pictures themselves but what is meant by them provides us with what we believe" (Glaube [1956], p. 518). In this case the fulfillment can also be in the form of a collective person. This is clearly what John has in mind when he sees the Antichrist in many antichrists. The fulfillment could also be thought of in this way, that the collective person will find his final expression in an individual person.

There are questions here which we cannot answer because Scripture does not give an answer. Scripture tells us that the Antichrist belongs to "the last hour" and is therefore there in some form at all times of the church's history. It is "the last time" ever since Christ, the Firstfruits, rose from the dead and so began the resurrection of all the dead (1 Cor. 15:23). It was already a part of the end of the world when Jerusalem, according to our Lord's prophecy, was destroyed in the year 70.

Only an utterly unbiblical way of looking at history could suppose that the Last Things belong altogether to the future, whether near or distant. As surely as the church never ceases to pray, "Thy kingdom come," and "Amen. Come, Lord Jesus," so surely it believes what the Lord says: "The hour is coming, and now is"(John 5:25), and also the warning of His apostle: "Children, it is the last hour" (1 John 2:18). Because this is so, the church knows that the Antichrist is in the world.

3

If it did not know about the mystery of the Antichrist, the church would not be able to exist. It would not be able to arm itself against him, to fight against him, to stand against him. When it is taught that the devil does not exist, he has achieved the propagation of his most dangerous triumph. Similarly there is no greater strengthening of the Antichrist than the view that he is only an apocalyptic figure who will later someday make his appearance—indeed a most sinister being, but nevertheless a useful warning before the end.

If the Antichrist is not yet on the scene, then the readying alarm has not yet been given. What an assurance of "All's well" is given by such thinking! This is true of the whole system of successive notifications which has been read out of Scripture: conversion of the Jews, resurrection of the martyrs, and so on. Those who think this way don't seem to realize that thereby the signs of the end, for which our Lord commanded us to watch, have been turned into their direct opposite. One may acknowledge that the Lord will come as a thief in the night, but one also knows that it is not yet night, even though it may be evening, and perhaps even late evening. The church will only be at the ready if it knows that the Antichrist is already in the world, and that it is at every moment exposed to the full force of his attacks. If it does not know this, then it is hopelessly defenseless against him. That is the meaning of the apostolic warnings.

What then is *the mystery of the Antichrist?* What does he want? What does he do? What he wants is to seduce Christians to fall away from the true God, the God revealed in Christ. In the place of the truth of the Gospel he puts the lie, the way of falsehood. Here the passages in John are in full agreement with 2 Thess. 2. And there is another point of complete agreement. In contrast with the devil, the Antichrist is religious. According to John he comes with a message which sounds quite Christian. He affirms the Gospel, but he falsifies it. According to 1 John 4:3 this falsification is done by denial of the Incarnation.

John was clearly writing vis-a-vis emerging Gnosticism. This powerful movement in the early days of Christianity was able to win over great numbers of Christians, notably in Egypt and Syria. In the middle of the second century the orthodox church, the church whose faith was in the incarnate Christ, appears to have been a minority. Yet in its way how pious was this honoring of Christ as a heavenly being that appeared here on earth with only the semblance of a body! Against this John wrote his gospel with its central theme: "The Word became flesh."

The religious character of the Antichrist, as described by Paul, is disclosed in the cult of man. This appears in the church, this religious exaltation of man. The voice of the serpent at the beginning in Paradise is heard again in the message of this Antichrist: "You will be as God." This is the oldest heresy in human history, and it appears in ever new forms to the end of the world. This is clearly the sense of the prophecy of the enemy who "exalts himself against every so-called god or object of worship, so that he takes his seat in the temple of God, proclaiming himself to be God" (2 Thess. 2:4).

Whatever forms this divinization of man may take in the future— and certainly such an error always gets worse—one would have to be struck blind not to recognize the appearance of this original heresy ever and again in Christian history. The natural man always has the inclination to use religion for his self-glorification, also the Christian religion. From ancient India we hear: "Atman is Brahman" (the soul is divine). Every missionary to India knows that the greatest hindrance to the Gospel is this divinization of man. This same divinization of man is to be found also in the idealism of the Greeks and of the Germans of the classical period, and it permeates the theology of the Greek fathers, of medieval scholasticism, and of modern Protestantism.

This is what the Antichrist wants. This is what he does. He leads men away from the worship of the one true God, the God who in Jesus Christ became flesh. He leads them to serve the human "I," exalted to the place of God. He does this from the days of the apostles down to the Last Day. This is something that happens in the church. Therefore the Antichrist is more dangerous than all other enemies of the church. No Roman caesar, no modern dictator is so dangerous as the enemy of Christ within the church.

When Pliny wrote to Trajan, he reported the measures he had taken against the Christians. These went so far as the execution of the "obstinate" ones who refused to recant. In the same letter he tells of Christians who had fallen away from the church 20 years previously. Such falling away in time of persecution is not the worst thing Christendom has experienced in this regard. This was recognized when the way of repentance was opened for those who had lapsed under pressure of persecution. It was the way the first denier, Simon Peter, had gone. Antichrist's great art is that he can bring Christians to fall away without persecution. When Islam was sweeping over Christians lands, there were Christians who almost clamored to become Moslems. Many of them could give religious reasons for doing so. The Islamic rulers even tried to forbid such conversions to Islam, or at least made them difficult, for the sake of the head-tax which Christians were required to pay. The highest art of the Antichrist is that he can make falling away a work of religious piety.

<h1 style="text-align:center">4</h1>

In Christian history there is no one who has so deeply probed the mystery of the Antichrist as Martin Luther, no one who so shuddered before it. In Roman theology, even in the greatest teachers of the Roman Church, the Antichrist has always appeared as a comparatively harmless being. This figure of the distant end time may indeed be painted with the most frightening colors, but one need not be too frightened when one knows that this monster will rule for "not too long" a time, that is, three and a half years (Scheeben-Atzberger, *Handbuch der katholischen Dogmatik*, IV, 904). It belongs to the essence of the Roman Church that it puts into a more or less distant future what Holy Scripture says about the events of the end time. For the present, then, Christians need not be much concerned about it.

For Luther the Antichrist was not so innocuous. Why did the Antichrist loom so large for him? Is this to be explained by the influence of the apocalypticism of the Late Middle Ages, nourished by a mood born of the feeling that a dying world was going under, as well as by the despair of pious people in regard to the ever-more-decadent church? This certainly was an influence upon Luther and upon the whole century of the Reformation. He, along with most of his contemporaries, was convinced of living in the eventide of the world. He never supposed that the world would last much longer. In his *On the Councils and the Church* he is prompted by Nicaea's Easter canon to speak of the planned reform of the Julian calendar, and he declares it unnecessary.

> What does it matter to us Christians? Even if our Easter should coincide with the day of St. Philip and St. James [May1] (which I hope will not happen before the end of the world) and move still further, we still celebrate Easter daily with our proclamation of Christ and our faith in him [WA 50,557; American Edition 41, 65].

Of the old calendar he says:

> The old garment with its great tear has stayed on and on, and now it may as well stay until the Last Day, which is imminent anyhow. Since the old garment has endured being patched and torn for approximately fourteen hundred years, it may as well let itself be patched and torn for another hundred years; for I hope that everything will soon come to an end [WA 50, 557; American Edition 41, 65].

Vilmar once said that it would have been better if Luther had not been so sure that the end of the world was about to happen. He would then have given more thought to the future of the church. Even if this be so, we must remember that Luther was not just captive to the way the Late Middle Ages thought about the world, but that more than any of his contemporaries he had immersed himself in the eschatology of the New Testament. For him, as for the church of the apostles, ecclesiology was a part of eschatology. Unlike the men of the 19th century who saw the church as one of the great social constructions of human history, he saw the church as the holy people of God of the end time, attacked by the devil, led by the Antichrist into the great temptation to fall away, and protected and preserved by Christ.

Therefore the Antichrist fills a far different role for Luther than for the men of the Middle Ages. He is not just a frightening figure who announces the Last Day; he is the great antagonist of Christ in the drama of the church's history. No one can know what the church is, what the kingdom of Christ is, who does not know the Antichrist. Therefore the Antichrist can only be understood from the vantage point of the Gospel, and not from that of the Law, as the Middle Ages tried to do. When the 12th century gave way to the 13th in the apocalyptically minded Middle Ages, there were voices to be heard, at first hesitatingly and softly, and then with mounting strength up to the days just before the Reformation, asking "whether the pope is the Antichrist." The reasons given for this thesis were always those of the Law. The pope was the guardian of God's law on earth, but he did not keep it; he cast it aside. He did not keep the law of Christ, for instance the command of poverty. He is the greatest and most frightful sinner of all because of his scandalous life, because of his greed and his tyranny.

Luther also knew of these sins and blamed the popes for them, but as Hans Preuss has observed: "An utterly scandalous life, no matter how bad, would never have persuaded him that the pope is the Antichrist" (*Vorstellungen vom Antichrist*, 1906, p. 152). Luther always warned the Evangelicals never to claim a higher level of morality than their opponents. We are all of us sinners, and there is no sense in quarreling about who is the biggest one. In his Table Talk Luther made a comparison between his battle with the pope and that of Wycliffe and Hus.

> Doctrine and life must be distinguished. Life is bad among us, as it is among the papists, but we don't fight about life and condemn the papists on that account. Wycliffe and Huss didn't know this and

attacked [the papacy] for its life. I don't scold myself into becoming good, but I fight over the Word and whether our adversaries teach it in its purity. That doctrine should be attacked—this has never before happened. This is my calling. . . . to treat doctrine is to strike at the most sensitive point . . . (WATR 1, 294 [American Edition 54,110]).

For Luther the pope is the Antichrist because his doctrine is anti-Christian. With his doctrine he casts the Lord Christ from His throne and puts himself there, there in the place which is Christ's alone. Christendom, then, must choose between the Gospel and the doctrine of the pope.

In light of this we can understand why Luther time and again spoke of his lifework as the battle against the papacy. He spoke of his room in the tower in Wittenberg as his "poor little room from which I stormed the papacy, and for that it is worthy of always being remembered." His thus identifying his lifework needs no more quotations, but we may note that he does this whenever he solemnly confesses his faith. So in the Great Confession of 1528, in the Smalcald Articles, and in the Brief Confession of 1544. For him to confess the Evangelical faith meant also to confess that the pope is the Antichrist. It pained him that this confession was missing in the Augsburg Confession. Hans Preus has pointed out that just in those hours when it seemed he was about to die he confessed his commitment to the battle against the pope as the Antichrist. In 1527, when he was very ill and expected to die, he was sad that he had not been found worthy of martyrdom, but he comforted himself with the fact that so it was even for St. John, who had written a "much harder" book against the Antichrist. Ten years later, when he was grievously ill at Smalcald, he said similar things. Finally, there is the gripping prayer he prayed the night of his death. He thanked God that He had made known to him His Son, "in whom I believe, whom I have preached and confessed, whom I have loved and praised, and whom the wretched pope and all the godless abuse, persecute and blaspheme" (cf. G. Köstlin, *Martin Luther*, Vol. II, 1903, pp. 170, 632; H. Preus, p. 146). Also in the wills which Luther made we find the thought expressed that the battle against the Antichrist was the battle of his life.

This battle cannot be explained by reference either to his temperament or to political motives. The former may apply at most to particular expressions which betray the irascibleness of an old man. These the Lutheran Church has rejected, as also have non-Lutheran critics who recognized them for what they were. The battle was not occasioned by moral outrage or by personal dislike. Of these we find more than enough

117

not only in the Late Middle Ages but also among good Catholics at the time of the Reformation. On the contrary, Luther had a sort of human sympathy for Leo X. The recognition that the pope is the Antichrist is for him much rather the other side of the knowledge of the Gospel, and the battle against the pope as the Antichrist is therefore the other side of the battle for the Gospel. To understand this profound connection is to understand what the Gospel is and who the pope is. Here is the reason why the Evangelical Lutheran Church accepts what (not how) Luther taught of the pope as Antichrist and why it proclaims in its Confessions as church doctrine that the pope is the Antichrist.

5

It should never have been questioned that this really is *church doctrine* and not merely a theological opinion of Luther's and of early Lutheran theology. On what grounds could one remove from the Confessions the large article on the Antichrist in the Smalcald Articles (II, IV)? The same is true of Apology VII and VIII, 24; XXIII, 25; XXIV, 51 (in all of which the German text uses the word "Antichrist," while Melanchthon's Latin text is content with citing Dan. 11) and in the Treatise on the Power and Primacy of the Pope, 39: "It is plain that the marks of the Antichrist coincide with those of the pope's kingdom and his followers." Yet if these passages are not in accord with Scripture, they should be removed. First, however, it would have to be shown that they are not in accord with Scripture, and second, if that were shown to be the case, the doctrine expressed there would have to be solemnly retracted before all the world.

One cannot, however, do it the way August Vilmar suggests: "That the pope in Rome is not the Antichrist, as used to be supposed in the Evangelical Church, is now so self-evident that any refutation of such an unclear notion is quite unnecessary and would indeed seem quite foolish" (*Dogmatik*, II, 306). Vilmar himself would likely have revised this statement, and many another which he wrote regarding the Roman Church, had he lived to witness Vatican I. That there may be no doubt about our position, let it be clearly said: A theologian who merely because it happens to be in the Confessions lets the doctrine stand that the pope is the Antichrist, and is not solidly convinced that it is so, cannot truthfully be called a Lutheran. He cannot escape the charge of slandering the papacy.

Why did the Lutheran Church accept Luther's teaching on this point? What is the meaning of this doctrine? We must first clearly recognize what the church did not accept. There were items in Luther's view of history which were not accepted, specifically that the end of the world would come not later than within the next century. With such presuppositions Luther could not possibly answer the question as to what new forms the Antichrist might assume in subsequent centuries. The church can have no doctrine which answers such a question. The church can and must teach that all the eschatological prophecies of Holy Scripture come to fulfillment. How that may happen lies beyond its knowing. We can never say with certainty how what Scripture says in apocalyptic picture language will be realized. The fulfillment of all prophecies is greater than could be grasped by those who heard them, even by those who heard them in faith. The Lutheran Church teaches nothing in its Confessions as to how God may let the prophecy of the Antichrist come to fulfillment in the hidden future, that is, what form the Antichrist may take in the final terrors of the end time. What our Confessions can teach, and do teach, this and no more, is that in the "last time" which we can see, in the time of the church until the present day, the prophecy of the Antichrist has found fulfillment in the papacy.

Luther himself never supposed that there was nothing to be seen of the Antichrist beyond the papacy. In his Great Confession of 1528 he says:

> The papacy is assuredly the true realm of Antichrist, the real anti-Christian tyrant, who sits in the temple of God and rules with human commandments, as Christ in Matthew 24 [:24] and Paul in II Thessalonians 2 [:3 f.] declare; although the Turk and all heresies, wherever they may be, are also included in this abomination which according to prophecy will stand in the holy place, but are not to be compared to the papacy (WA 26, 507 [American Edition 37, 367 f.]).

This always remained his conviction, and Lutheran theology always followed him in this matter.

But why is the pope the "true" Antichrist? The Smalcald Articles give the following answer:

> [He] has raised himself over and set himself against Christ, for the pope will not permit Christians to be saved except by his own power, which amounts to nothing since it is neither established nor commanded by God. This is actually what St. Paul calls exalting oneself over and against God (II, IV, 10).

It is really unnecessary to quote the passages in which overzealous devotees of the pope have predicated of him what belongs only to God.

119

This they did and were not excommunicated for it. Among them were the medieval canonists Augustine of Ancona and Zenzelinus of Cassanis. (Documentation is given [in Tappert, p. 300, and] in *Bekenntnisschriften*, p. 431.) Among them also were the Ultramontanists of the 19th century who so flattered Pius IX. What the Confessions teach is that when the pope promulgates a dogmatic decision, one which has no basis in Holy Scripture, and makes men's salvation or damnation depend on their obedience or disobedience toward it, then he is setting himself in the place of Christ, in the place of God. This is what Luther, with sharp prophetic vision, saw as the essence of the papacy, even though he could not yet know the Council of Trent or Vatican I.

If there was any doubt on the part of some Lutherans as to the correctness of Luther's judgment, then this was removed when Pius IX, with the consent of the Vatican Council, on 18 July 1870 promulgated the constitution *Pastor aeternus*. In it eternal salvation was denied to those who consciously oppose the dogma that the pope has the exercise of direct episcopal power over the whole church, over the infallibility with which Christ has equipped His church, and that his *ex cathedra* decisions in questions of faith and morals are, "of themselves, and not from the consensus of the church," true and irreformable (*ex sese, non autem ex consensu Ecclesiae irreformabiles* [Denzinger 3074]). And when the first of these new *ex cathedra* decisions was proclaimed—the dogma of the Assumption of Mary, in 1950, on All Saints' Day, the day inseparably connected with the Reformation—the shock wave hit all Christendom. Here became visible something of the reality which Luther had recognized with deep dread—the reality of the man who puts himself in God's place and proclaims his fantasies as divine revelation.

The pope is either Christ's vicar or he is the Antichrist. That is the alternative which Luther recognized quite clearly. Either the papacy is indeed instituted by God or it is an institution "instituted by the devil" (Luther: *vom Teufel gestiftet*). This institution is not merely human. It is more than a heretical institution. It is also something fundamentally different from the great non-Christian powers. They launch their attacks against the Christian faith from the outside, and will continue to do so. Whatever devilish attacks may be made against the church by the fearful totalitarian powers of the world, no representative of these powers has yet claimed to be Christ's vicar and to speak and act in His name. They set up their temple next to the church and seek to displace it. In the papacy, however, the man who deifies himself has worked his way into the church. This is what is so horrendous in the papacy.

120

And since 1870 the church, insofar as it has placed itself under the papacy, can never get free of this. Not only are the dogmas which the pope produces irreformable (among them the constitution *Pastor aeternus*), but there is no power above him. "No one shall judge the supreme see." This fundamental law is adduced in the Treatise on the Power and Primacy of the Pope (50) as evidence of the anti-Christian character of the papacy. It is now set in concrete in Canon 1556 of the Codex of Canon Law (*Codex iuris canonici*). No council can ever judge the pope or in any way stand over him. If the pope dies during an ecumenical council, the council is at the moment of his death interrupted, and can only be begun again, or not begun again, by the new pope (Canon 229, *Codex iuris canonici*). Both according to [canon] law and according to the doctrine of the Roman Church, this institution can never be removed from the church or be deprived of its claims. Of all the great persecutions which Christianity has endured, those words apply which we hear from the faith of the ancient church, "It is a little cloud; it will pass." Of the sinister temptation which the Antichrist is for the church, it can only be said that he will continue until the returning Christ destroys him.

6

In Letter No. 13, "Is the Pope Really Still the Antichrist?" we pointed out, over against the position taken by Hans Asmussen, that the papacy today is essentially the same as the papacy which confronted Luther. Responses came also from some Roman Catholic readers of that letter. Among them was a venerable Jesuit Father [Cardinal Bea] who for decades has worked for better understanding between our confessions. They sought to persuade the writer that a revision of the old Lutheran judgment of the papacy is made necessary simply by the fact that a common front of all Christian churches is called for against the militant atheism of modern Communism. And it is a widely held notion that the judgment of Luther and the Confessions on this point is only of temporary significance, that it cannot be maintained in the modern world if only because the papacy is not in the hands of such morally vulnerable characters as in the time of Luther. At that time one may have observed the power of "lawlessness" [2 Thess. 2:3], whereas nowadays, on the contrary, the papacy is a stronghold of God's law and the Christian religion. It has also been said that the first pope to die a martyr's death will put an end to the talk about the pope being the Antichrist. Now we must respond to these objections.

121

Concerning the morals of the popes, Luther long since put an end to the notion that here are the grounds for recognizing the pope as the Antichrist.

As to the papacy being the guardian of God's law and the Christian religion in the modern world, it all depends on what is meant by law and by Christian religion. We have already observed that it is hardly by chance that the great, bloody revolutions took place in Catholic lands. The Catholic countries of Europe and South America have tumbled from one revolution to another. There seems to be only one Catholic king left in the world, in Belgium, and his throne is none too sure. What of Russia? One cannot call it a Protestant country. The mausoleum of Lenin stands next to the Chapel of the Iberian Madonna—a warning as to where the path of giving reverence to men can lead, even if it begins in the refined rites of the cult of Mary. Whoever knows the inner history of Europe's Catholic countries, in particular of the ecclesiastical principalities, and above all of the Papal States, will recognize the fearful consequences for God's church of not having heeded the Lutheran Reformation's warning against mixing church and state—something that can also be observed in the Lutheran Church itself.

The statement that the papacy is the stronghold of God's law in the world has its context in the confusion and ignorance of the modern world as to what is law given by God. Is it to be regarded as divine law that the supposed vicar of Christ makes the demand that all mankind shall be obedient to him in all decisions concerning faith and morals? Don't people see that here we have the source of the totalitarian systems of our day?

Mussolini and Hitler were sons of the Roman Church. Stalin even got as far as candidate of theology. There have certainly been absolute states before, and they came out of Spain and France. Modern totalitarianism is characterized by its claim to have power over the souls of men. This was not so in the world empires of antiquity. A citizen had indeed to go along with the state cult, but he was left to think about it what he liked. That souls can be compelled to a faith, that was first discovered by Catholicism, and secular imitators of the Roman Catholic church-system have made use of this discovery. Without an infallible pope there would never have been an infallible Hitler. The total state was born along with the total church on July 18, 1870.

How deep this connection is can be seen in the history of the last generation, whose documents are now more and more coming out of the archives. Fascism could not have happened in Italy without the pope.

The history of the '30s reveals how close was the tie between them, as well as what all was included in the Lateran treaties. The moral responsibility for all the horrors of the Abyssinian war, if it can be called a war, is shared by the Vatican. And it was not only the Madonna of Fatima who rescued the Iberian Peninsula from Bolshevism or what was so called.

We Germans who lived through it, those who had their eyes open in the fateful year of our people, the fearful year 1933, know who it was that helped Hitler to power. Without that help he would not have came to power except by violent revolution. It was not only the foolish Evangelical pastors, not only the decadent German citizenry, but the Vatican that did this. To the horror of thinking German Catholics, the Vatican ordered the dissolution of the Center Party because National Socialism was needed for the struggle against the East. For that the German people were sacrificed. Then, to be sure, when the concordat was broken (that gentlemen's agreement between two parties of whom each was convinced that the other was no gentleman), and it became clear in Rome that the stronger cards were in the other hand, then all of a sudden there was staunch defense of the very holy human rights which had not long ago been betrayed to Hitler.

We mention these things here only to refute the pious legend that the papacy is the stronghold of civil order and God's law in the world. The Roman Church is the continuation of the Roman Empire with other instrumentalities. It is the empire in the form of a church, at bottom a synthesis of church and world, of divine and human, and therefore it is that temple where man has put himself on the throne of God.

The Roman Church is indeed the defender of the Christian religion, but of what sort? In this Christian religion God is not the only Lord who is served. Our Lord Christ said clearly that one cannot serve two lords. Putting another lord beside Him, or another lady, like Mary Queen of Heaven, has in it a fatal propensity to displace Him. In theory it sounds fine when it is said that grace is superior to nature and the human will, Christ to His mother, the Redeemer to the coredemptrix, the single Mediator of the New Testament to the mediatrix of all graces. But when Catholic people are taught that the way to Christ is by way of Mary, then she has practically become the savior. Then one has to say of the pope as Luther did in his last confession: "What good does it do him greatly to exalt with his mouth the true God, the Father, the Son, and the Holy Spirit, and to make a splendid pretense of living a Christian life?" (*Brief Confession Concerning the Holy Sacrament*, 1544 [WA 54,

160; American Edition 38, 310]). But we have already discussed this aspect of Catholicism in Letter No. 13, and so need not repeat what was said there of the organic connection of the institution of the papacy with synergistic doctrine and the cult of Mary.

Only one thing more. A modern pope simply cannot be a martyr for the Christian faith like the old bishops of Rome. He would die not only for faith in Christ, but at the same time also for the superstition of Fatima; not only for the doctrine of the Gospel, but at the same time also for those errors which have been proclaimed as divine revelations necessary for salvation, such as the dogmas of the Immaculate Conception and of the Assumption of Mary, and the universal episcopacy and infallibility of the pope. He would die also for the false claim that he is Christ's vicar on earth, to whom every human being, on pain of losing his salvation, owes obedience in all dogmatic decisions, as though to the Lord Himself. This is what has to be said to those who maintain that Luther's judgment on the papacy is no longer current.

7

Among theologians it should not be necessary to spend many words to make it clear that the judgments which the Confessions of our church make about the papacy are statements of theology and doctrine, the opposite of those outbursts against individual popes and against the Roman Church that are produced by human anger and hatred. Luther's judgment against the pope has nothing to do with that of French or Italian Freemasons. It is also quite different from that of German politicians who from time to time tell of the injuries done the German people from the end of the time of the Staufers [13th century] up to the present. The judgment of the Lutheran Confessions is also something quite different from what was heard from German Protestantism during the *Kulturkampf* [in the 1870s], from the Evangelical League in Germany, from the Away-from-Rome movement in Austria [early 20th century], or from the anti-Rome movement in the United States unleashed by the proposal that the United States have an ambassador to the Holy See. What do any of these movements know of the Antichrist? They can know nothing of the Antichrist, for they do not know what the Gospel is and what the means of grace are, which have been given by Christ.

It was Luther's deep understanding of the Gospel that enabled him on the one hand to recognize its fearful perversion in the papacy, and on the other hand to give a positive evaluation of those elements of the true church of Christ that still live on in the Roman Church. The same Smalcald Articles which so sharply delineate the doctrine of the Antichrist also acknowledge that "the sublime articles of the divine majesty" "are not matters of dispute or contention," and give a considerable list of those matters which they wish to discuss with the Roman theologians. In the eyes of the world, which knows not the Gospel, this is an inexplicable contradiction. To understand it, one must know much about the reality of the church—of the church as Christ's kingdom which must always struggle against the kingdom of the devil in this last and evil time.

It is not only human beings who are engaged in this drama. It was not only Eugenio Pacelli who proclaimed the false doctrine of the Assumption of Mary as a revelation given to Christianity. It was not actually and not alone Giovanni Medici who cast Luther out of the church. It was not actually Alexander Farnese who repudiated *sola fide* and so also the Lord Christ Himself. Rather it was the Antichrist who spoke and acted in and through them. For this reason we, as also Luther did, can have some human, sympathetic understanding for those men who bore the fearful office of the papacy. This is especially true in the case of those popes who, as far as human eyes can see, were noble figures in the history of the papacy.

As did our fathers before us, so we too know ourselves to be bound together in the one holy church of Christ with all those who live within the true church also in the Roman Church—those who are born of the means of grace, the Gospel and the sacraments, which have not yet entirely perished in the Roman Church. We Lutherans should also be shamed by the true and living faith in Christ that is present within the Roman Church in spite of the Antichrist and his seductive wiles. In the Roman Church there are Christians who truly live from the Gospel that is still there, from the Gospel in the prayer in the Canon of the Mass itself, "not judging our merits, but forgiving our iniquities." We know of Christians there who, when it came to die, knew nothing save Christ and Him crucified, and who died in faith in Him, forgetting about the whole churchly apparatus and the world of saints: "King of majesty tremendous, Who dost free salvation send us, Fount of pity, then befriend us" [*The Lutheran Hymnal*, 607:8]. To recognize this is to see why Luther laid such weight on the fact that the Antichrist would not be the Antichrist unless he were actually seated "in the temple," the church of God.

We are aware, honored brethren, of what a responsibility we take upon ourselves when we today repeat in such a way the old doctrine of the Lutheran Church concerning the pope as the Antichrist. We know that we shall have to answer for this before the judgment seat of Him who someday will judge the claims of all churches, the doctrine of all confessions. His judgment is the decisive one for us, not the opinions of men.

The majority of Western Christians today, and their theologians, including Lutheran ones, show no knowledge of this doctrine of the Reformation. And why is this? Because our generation has to a large extent lost any grasp of the great realities of the faith. One is struck here in Australia, on the edge of the Asiatic world, when meeting Christians from the "younger churches" of the mission fields, by how entirely different is their relationship to the New Testament and to the realities given us there. For them this is all new, fresh, and alive, while for us Europeans or Americans it is covered with a layer of dust centuries thick. The Epistles and Gospels which are read in church on Sunday we already know, or think we know. The hymns we sing once poured out of hearts made glad by the newly discovered Gospel—but that was long ago.

Here lies the deepest reason why Luther's doctrine of the Antichrist has become strange to us. One must know much about the reality of Christ, about His real presence, about His actions, dealings, and sufferings in today's world, in order to see the Antichrist in his manifold appearances, also the most splendid and powerful ones. One must literally live from the Gospel as the message of the sinner's justification in order to know what it means to exclude this Gospel from the church in the name of Christ and to deny salvation to those who teach, believe, and confess it.

God grant us all, pastors and congregations, teachers and students of theology, open eyes and an ever deeper understanding of His Word, and thereby an ever clearer view of the reality of the Antichrist, wherever and in whatever form we may encounter him, even if it be in our own Lutheran Church!

With this wish I greet you, dear brothers in the ministry, in these Easter days, in the unity of the faith.

THE CHURCH LIVES!
A Sermon on Acts 2:42-47 for the First Sunday After Trinity

June 27, 1943

When this war is finally over, then the question will be heard again, echoing over the scorched earth and through the exhausted people of the West: "What about the church of God?" Thus it has always been when a great war had thoroughly devastated the natural fellowships of birth and history. So it was after the Thirty Years' War, after the Napoleonic wars, and after the First World War. At such times Christians have remembered what they confess Sunday by Sunday before the altar: "I believe in the holy Christian church, the communion of saints." What kind of a reality is meant by this? Whoever has ears to hear already perceives this question struggling to be heard in the world and among our German people.

Yes, what sort of a reality stands behind this confession? Perhaps none at all? Is it perhaps just an old formula that has lost any meaning, when in the midst of the most dreadful of all wars, which has long since stopped being an honorable, knightly battle, when in the midst of this war, Sunday after Sunday, yes day after day, the confession is made in a thousand languages: "I believe in the Holy Spirit, the holy Christian church, the communion of saints"?

No, it is no mere formula. Here is a reality. It may, to be sure, be overlooked or forgotten. It may be hidden from our eyes as is the sun when it has gone down in the evening sky. But it is a reality that is still there, as surely as the sun which has set is still there, even if our eyes do not see it. No, it is much more sure than that. For whether the sun will rise again tomorrow, that I cannot know with certainty. But that God the Father, the almighty Creator of heaven and earth, is still there—that I surely know. That Jesus Christ is Lord, to whom all power has been given in heaven and on earth, that the Holy Spirit, who proceeds from the Father and the Son, moves over the chaos of this time as He did in the beginning over the dark depths—that I know. And therefore I also know that there exists the church of which the creed speaks: the church which is the people of God, the body of Christ, the temple of the Holy Spirit. What better place can there be for deepening our understanding of the reality of the church than where the church first makes its appearance before our eyes in human history, at least insofar as it can be seen by our eyes?

So God's church comes before our eyes in our text which brings to an end the great Pentecost chapter in the Acts of the Apostles. The scene begins with the Pentecost miracle, followed by Peter's sermon and the baptism of the 3,000. Then the life of the congregation is described in a few matter-of-fact words, and yet they vibrate with what happened in the transforming events of those days: the inexpressible joy of the newly baptized, the simplicity of faith with which they devoted themselves to the apostles' teaching, the awe of their hearts before the wonders of the Spirit, the brotherly love which is ready to offer everything, the prayers, the celebrations of the Sacrament, and the praise of God.

It is not difficult to see why this text has always been so profoundly moving, and has prompted so much in the history of the church. The way it has stirred people may be compared with the account of the rich young ruler, which ever and again has turned people around and brought them to the commitment of all their earthly possessions. So also Jesus' charge to the Twelve as He sent them out (Matt. 10) was ever and again used as a mirror in which the church of the Middle Ages recognized its sin and apostasy. So then also what Luke reports of the first congregation in Acts 2 and 4 has been heard ever and again since the early days of the church as a call to repentance. "They devoted themselves to the apostles' teaching and fellowship, to the breaking of bread and the prayers." And we? "All who believed were together and had all things in common." And we? " . . . continuing daily with one accord . . . " [KJV]. And we? ". . . with glad and generous hearts, praising God . . ." And we? Such questioning has ever and again been prompted by the account of the first congregation, and so it must be. Here a mirror is held up to the church of all times, a call to repentance.

It is this only, however, when it is rightly understood. It can be misunderstood, just as the account of the rich young ruler and Jesus' charge to the Twelve have been misunderstood. It is understood falsely

128

when one sees in it only Law. How often this has happened! [People have said that] the church today should be as it was then, and therefore we must again make it like that. How often in the history of the church has the attempt been made to copy it! We see it in the Anabaptists at the time of the Reformation, in the Philadelphian societies and other fellowship constructions of Pietism, in Irving's Catholic Apostolic Church in England, in the large Disciples of Christ denomination in America. There seems to be no end to the sects and fellowships which make this attempt.

The view is widely held among them that in the original church all property was held in common, a sort of noble communism. The New Testament tells us nothing of this. In the case of Ananias and Sapphira we are told explicitly that everyone could keep his property if he wished. There was no law. What we are told is that no one said of his property that it was his. Rather, they disposed what they had for the benefit of others, for those who were poorer. We are told that "they (not all) sold their possessions and goods and distributed them to all, as any had need"—a sort of common chest. Probably these were those who came from Galilee to Jerusalem to await Christ's return. Of the mother of John Mark, who wrote our oldest Gospel, we are told in Acts 12 that she owned a house in Jerusalem.

The idea of communism (mark well, the communism of love, which does not say, "What is thine is mine," but rather "What is mine is thine") is a very idealistic notion. And this ideal is read into the account in Acts. It then becomes an example to be emulated by organizing Christian associations in which private property is abolished. What eventuates can be seen in some of the saddest stories in church history: congregations that began as a fellowship of Jesus ending up as a synagogue of Satan.

The urge to make a copy of the original church has prompted some to fasten on "they devoted themselves to the apostles' teaching . . . and many wonders and signs were done through the apostles." How can a copy be made of the original church without its most important office, the office of the apostles? Therefore let us make some new apostles! Such is the folly arrived at in England in the last century by Edward Irving. So first there was the Catholic Apostolic Church, and later another one called the New Apostolic Church.

Or it could go like this: In the original church the Christians were not called Lutherans or Reformed, Presbyterians or Congregationalists, Methodists or Baptists, Catholics or Orthodox. They were called dis-

129

ciples. So let us have a church of the Disciples of Christ. Such was the thinking of a pious American pastor a hundred years ago. Disciples of Christ is what all Christians want to be. Here is quite the simplest way, then, to overcome the divisions of Christianity. But naturally this movement also did not renew the one church, but only made another new one, even though very large and respectable. If I should attempt, my dear Christian hearers, to give you only a sketch of all such attempts, we would still be sitting here in church at noon. All these fellowships resulted from attempts to understand and obey our text as a law for the renewal of the church.

Our text is perverted when it is used as a law for shaping the life of the church. When men do that, they end up where all men of the Law end up—either in deep despair or in titanic arrogance.

Many, many Christians have ended in deep despair, because they did not attain the blessed state of this first congregation. I remember such a one from the time when I was serving as a pastor in Berlin. He was a popular preacher, something of a revivalist, who had the gift of giving his testimony of the Lord Christ to mass gatherings of Berlin workers. He had at one time, as a Red sailor and as a member of the Soldiers' Council in Kiel, participated in the revolution. Then he was converted to the Christian faith and became a missionary at large (*Volksmissionar*). He wanted to reform the church by turning into reality what was said of the original church. This man finally went to Russia and became a Bolshevist agitator. He had despaired of being able to renew the church today according to the model of the original church, and so to reform it.

The other way things go with men of the Law is the titanic arrogance of those who imagine that it will be easy to renew the church in the ideal form of the church at its beginning. The arrogance which here comes to expression is a hidden or unspoken faith in man. It should not be hard [they say] to be and to achieve what the first congregation was and achieved. The first Christians were only men, but what splendid men they were! Men of such splendid faith, men of such splendid brotherly love! What can hinder us from being such as they?

What hinders us is the same as hindered them. This is something we must be quite clear about, dear congregation, if we would be honest and not a prey to false illusions. As at all times, so also in that first time the church was a little group of poor sinners. If you want to understand the original church and its meaning for the church of all times, then you must first recognize that they were such as we are, poor sinners. They had no other strengths than we have. They were no better than the Christians of all times. If they were holy, then it was not in any other way than that way in which poor sinners at any time are holy—holy by the fact that Christ died for their sins. He was made "our wisdom, our righteousness and sanctification and redemption" [1 Cor. 1:30]. Our wisdom is Christ. Our righteousness is Christ. Our sanctification is Christ. Our redemption is Christ. So it was in the first congregation, a congregation of nothing but poor sinners.

So the New Testament tells of it. It was the congregation in which the wicked case of Ananias and Sapphira could happen. It was the congregation, as we are told in Acts 6, in which, in spite of love communism, in spite of the splendid caring for the poor, it could happen that "the Hellenists murmured against the Hebrews because their widows were neglected in the daily distribution." The first quarrel in the first congregation was about money, about how it was allotted from the church's treasury. There was, if one may say so, something not quite straight in the way the gifts collected in the congregation were being allotted.

Then follow the controversies in the church between Paul and Barnabas, between Paul and the first congregation, between Paul and Peter, and then between Paul and Peter on the one side and James on the other. And so it goes on and on in the early church. No, the early church was anything but a church of saints who are to serve as examples of splendid Christians to be emulated through all subsequent centuries. The church of the first century is a communion of saints in the same sense as the church of every century: It is a congregation of justified sinners. The first Christians also lived from nothing else than the daily forgiveness of their sins, as we confess in the Small Catechism: "In this Christian church he daily and abundantly forgives all my sins, and the sins of all believers." The holiness of the church is the holiness of Christ. We correctly understand what our text tells us about what happened in the first church, the congregation of saints in Jerusalem, when we hear not the praise of men but only "Holy, holy, holy is the Lord," the everlasting song of the church: "You only are holy; You only are the Lord; You only . . . are Most High."

So the church is never something made or put together by pious people, but it is the church of the Lord Christ. Not in the religion which men do, even if it is the highest and most beautiful blossoming of human religious activity, not in the faith of a Peter or a Paul does the church's glory have its source. Of that source we are told in our text: "They devoted themselves to the apostles' teaching and fellowship, to the breaking of bread and the prayers." Doctrine of the apostles, fellowship, breaking of bread, prayers—in these four things is hidden the secret of the church.

"They devoted themselves to the apostles' teaching." They did not grow tired of hearing the words spoken by the apostles, the witness to Jesus Christ, His incarnation, His deeds and words, and that He "died for our sins in accordance with the Scriptures, that He was buried, that He was raised on the third day in accordance with the Scriptures." In these words, transmitted by Paul (1 Cor. 15:3–4), we have the oldest formulations of the apostolic proclamation, the first steps of the later creeds: ". . . dead, and buried . . . the third day he rose from the dead." That was the doctrine of the apostles. That was what they repeated day by day.

"We are witnesses to all that He did both in the country of the Jews and in Jerusalem. They put Him to death by hanging Him on a tree; but God raised Him on the third day and made Him manifest; not to all the people but to us who were chosen by God as witnesses, who ate and drank with Him after He rose from the dead" (Acts 10, 39–41). It was always the same message, repeated with sublime monotony by the apostles, who were eyewitnesses, and then after their death by those to whom the apostolic proclamation was committed. The church of all times lives from the doctrine of the apostles.

But does it really? Must not the church adjust its message to the contemporary situation? The reproach of not moving with the times was heard in Germany through the 18th and 19th centuries from those who held a naive faith in progress. Why go on preaching the same as Peter did in the Acts of the Apostles? How many theologians, indeed whole churches, finally had enough! They did not continue in the apostles' doctrine. They preached something else. Forty years ago they preached sermons on Goethe and Schiller. They preached the current view of the world, although most world views are lucky if they last as long as 30 years. And the churches did not become fuller, but emptier. And rightly so. For since 1848 any member of German society could read in the newspaper every morning as he drank his coffee what the latest and only acceptable world view is. For this I do not need to go to church. But where the church continued in the apostles' doctrine, there the congregation remained.

To the world it is inexplicable that the church lives on, always preaching the same old thing. In fact, it is because the same old thing goes on being preached, the apostles' doctrine, that the church goes on living. This is because the apostles' doctrine is the everlasting Word of God to all men, to all nations, to all times. It is the Gospel of Jesus Christ, the eternal Son of God, "who for us men and for our salvation came down from heaven . . . and was made man." He "was put to death for our trespasses and raised for our justification" [Rom. 4:25]. He "is seated at the right hand of the Father . . . and His kingdom shall have no end." The apostolic doctrine witnesses to the Word of God become flesh. In this witness, in the simple words of the apostles, in the straightforward words preached in the church, Christ, the eternal Word, is Himself present. *Therefore* the church lives from the apostolic doctrine.

"They devoted themselves to the apostles' teaching and fellowship." Also in this word "fellowship" something of the deep, divine mystery of the church lies hidden. For this word means something else than what we human beings otherwise call fellowship. Of human fellowship we have two kinds. There is the natural fellowship into which we are born. This is there before we are, and we are born into it without our consent. Such is the fellowship of our family and people. Then there is the fellowship which occurs because we wish it to, a fellowship we enter voluntarily. There is such a fellowship when we more or less voluntarily join a gymnastics club, a party, an association that has a purpose with which we sympathize.

But the fellowship which binds together the members of the church never arises in such a way. We are not born into the church, nor can we join it. These are two very serious misunderstandings. "Those who received his word"—the words of Peter's Pentecost sermon having gone into them working faith—"were baptized, and there were added that day about three thousand souls" [Acts 2:41]. They "were baptized"— passive voice. They "were added"—passive voice. The One who added them was the One who called them by the Gospel and kindled the light of faith in their hearts.

In this way, and in no other, did we also become members of the church. You also were added by the Holy Spirit when you were baptized. Baptism is not some symbolic action, an initiation rite done or devised by men. It is a sacrament of Jesus Christ. And in the sacraments God is already now at this time doing something with us which He plans to do at the end of all things. In a sacrament the future becomes a present reality; it is eternity that has become time. So it is in Holy Absolution, as that doctrine is confessed in our church. Already now the forgiving words, which free us from sin, speak to us the verdict of the Final Judgment. So in Holy Communion we are given the fellowship of the body and blood of Christ, which will not come to consummation until the end of all things.

Your resurrection began when you were baptized. "We were buried therefore with Him [Christ] by baptism into death, so that as Christ was raised from the dead by the glory of the Father, we too might walk in newness of life" (Rom. 6:4). With Christ you died at that time, with Him you were buried, with Him you shall rise. With Him, for you have been made a member of His body. That is the deep secret of the fellowship of the saints. So we, "though many, are one body. . . . For by one Spirit we were all baptized into one body" (1 Cor. 12:12–13). And again: "Because there is one bread, we who are many are one body, for we all partake of the one bread" (1 Cor. 10:17). That is certainly a fellowship which the world does not know and can never understand. It is the imperishable communion of saints.

Perhaps some of you are thinking that this is all some theological theory, some theology pushed too far. Such thoughts come to us because we are children of the modern world, which no longer knows of the profound reality of the living Christ. The church of which our text speaks knew about it. It lived thereby. Our fathers in the church of the Reformation also lived thereby. Whatever there is of genuine, deep brotherly love in the church of all times has grown out of this love. Let me mention only one instance, that of the church's loving service (*Diakonie*). This was the ancient church's claim to fame, even among the heathen. "See, how they love one another!" There was then such a caring for the poor and the sick, for the lonely and helpless, as the world had never known before. For the ancient civilization was a civilization without mercy, just as our world is threatening to again become a world without mercy. But all that loving activity would never have happened without the Lord's Supper. For all loving service proceeds from the altar. So it was in the early church, when the deacons and deaconesses brought the consecrated bread and wine to the sick, the lonely, the helpless, those who could not come to church. With this they brought along the congregation's gifts of love, and thereby the comfort, the help, and the fellowship of the Christian brotherhood. When in the 19th century there was a revival of the Christian diaconate, we again see such loving service going out from the altar. In Neuendettelsau the deaconess houses became places of renewed liturgy and renewed celebration of Holy Communion. You have only to attend a divine service in Bethel [a well-known home for the handicapped at Bielefeld, Germany] to realize why

Father Bodelschwingh [its founder] maintained the Lutheran liturgy with such great faithfulness.

But the diaconate is only one evidence of the profound connection between the sacraments and the works of practical service in the communion of saints, that communion which is inexplicable to any human reason, because it is the fellowship of the body of Christ. This fellowship goes with Holy Communion, which in our text is called by its ancient code name, "the breaking of bread." ". . . breaking bread in their homes"—they had no other place for this. "They devoted themselves to the apostles' teaching and fellowship, to the breaking of bread. . . ." These together.

For the church today, and also our Lutheran Church, there is nothing more needful than pondering this fact. When fellowship is separated from Holy Communion both are diminished. Today Holy Communion has been pushed into the background—the celebration which was the core of the divine service for all Christians until the Reformation, and still was so in the first two centuries of the Evangelical Lutheran Church. Now we often find that it has been removed from the service. Certainly not every member of the congregation can or should receive Communion every Sunday, but the Sacrament is to be celebrated in its midst.

But is there not a danger of this becoming one of those laws that ever and again have been taken from our text? No, this is no law, no more than the admonition to continue in the apostles' doctrine and the fellowship, and to be steadfast in prayer. Also *prayer*—our text uses the plural—is profoundly connected with the celebration of the Lord's Supper. Without these prayers, without the joy and rejoicing of the congregation overflowing with thanksgiving, without the irrepressible praise of what great and marvelous things the Lord has done, without the worship of the present Lord Christ, there can be no church.

They praised God "with glad and generous hearts." All liturgy of the church, all praying of the church, is only an echo of this praise of God, of these soaring-to-heaven prayers of Christianity's first Pentecost season. Then the Spirit of God enlivened hearts, enabling them to pray. For it is true also of the church that "we do not know how to pray as we ought, but the Spirit Himself intercedes for us with sighs too deep for words" (Rom. 8:26). And not in vain do we call upon the Holy Spirit as follows:

You are the Spir't who teaches
How one should pray aright.
Your prayers are ever answered,

135

Your songs are ever bright.
To heav'n goes up Your call,
And for our help is pleading,
Till He the help is giving,
Whose aid is there for all.

The picture of the first church given in our text is a gripping picture indeed. But we must not forget that the light which shines about the first congregation in Jerusalem is not only the daybreak red of the church's morning, but also the sunset red of an earthly people. They were a perishing people, and a generation later that judgment was fulfilled which goes out over every nation that rejects Christ. The Jewish Christian congregation fled across the Jordan, prompted by a prophetic utterance. Their role was over, bound up with the history of their people.

But Christ's church did not come to an end. The call of God's Holy Spirit went out to the peoples of the heathen world, and then they in their day were alive with the truth of these words: "They devoted themselves to the apostle's teaching and fellowship, to the breaking of bread and the prayers." Nations pass away, but the church continues. And where there is a people which no longer has a future, there the church still has a future, because the future of the church is the future of Jesus Christ. Amen.